ALL STEAMED UP

A STORY OF REAL EVENTS

AROUND THE READING GREAT WESTERN LOCO DEPOT IN THE 1950s AND 1960s AS THE STEAM ERA CAME TO AN END.

BY JAMES H BRIGGS

READING LOCO DEPOT 1930s ERA

2898 AT OXFORD LOCO DEPOT

ALF BOTTIN TIPPING A COAL TUB ONTO 7903

LAMBOURNE BRANCH TRAIN

4995 AT THE REAR OF THE LOCO SHED

The steam train era lasted a longer time in Great Britain than it did in Europe. The modernisation of railways in Europe went ahead fast after WW2. The diesel engines and overhead electrics were way ahead of Great Britain. The need for railway staff was paramount to keep the railways running in the 1950s and 60s. But the public demanded cleaner working conditions, and staff were harder to employ and keep. The steam railways would never be able to comply with the Health and Safety Act if the steam era was to go on, so the steam era ended in 1964.

The steam age was adventurous and sometimes exciting for the staff. The steam engines such as the GWR Kings, Castles and Hall class were superb engines to fire and drive. My short employment with British Rail was from 1955 to 1963. This book is a short story of the cleaners, firemen and drivers I had the pleasure to work with. I consider the time I spent on the footplate was a very good learning curve for a young man as I worked with mature men, some due to retire. Each man had a history and the tales they related still stay fresh in my mind. Some fought in WW1 and had tales of the trenches. One driver related to me the time he fought in WW2 and was captured at Dunkirk in 1940. He said he fell asleep on the beach with exhaustion and when he awoke a big German soldier stood over him with a bayonet pointed his way. He spent 5 years as a prisoner of war. When anyone mentioned they were going to Spain for a holiday he used to go into a fit of bitterness, after all he spent over 5 years in Europe. This and the things I relate in this book are true day-to-day events of the steam age.

We started work at the age of 15 years and by the time we had grown out of our teens we were considered old hand firemen. The pictures I have put in the book are scenes of the locomotive shed in Great Knollys Street and other areas around Reading where we worked. I am sure there are relatives of the people I mention still living in the Reading area and they should be proud of the fact that if it was not for the efforts and integrity of these men the railway would not have functioned.

I have read many good books about the steam era but not many mention or explain what it was like to experience the hardships, the pride and the comradeship of working on the footplate. I have tried to explain the methods used to keep the steam engines functioning, how the drivers had their different methods of driving these living steam breathing beasts. To me the steam engine was a living beast. You feed it coal after lighting a fire in its belly. When it comes alive you have to feed it water to keep it alive. Take away its fire and water and it dies or becomes a dormant beast awaiting someone to bring it back to life. Well, reader, I hope you get pleasure from reading this short narrative and perusing the pictures - all history now.

THE INTERVIEWS

He sat in the classroom and tried to think of what to say to the careers master. He was 15 years old without a clue of what type of job he wanted. Slight of build and not very athletic he considered a job as a telegram boy with the post office to be a good idea. Riding around on a motorbike and being paid for it. Bloody ace that job. He brushed his hand through his dark hair and straightened his tie. Got to took posh ain't you, for an interview, he thought. Although his light beige coloured bomber jacket was covered in ink stains, caused by acting the fool with his mates. He had the interview but it did no bloody good because the careers bloke said he would have to stay at school for another year! The reason being that you could not ride a motorbike legally until you were 16 years old. Bugger that he thought, not another year at school, while all his mates were working. Not an option, no bloody way. So he made his way home and dejectedly told his parents that the interview was a load of rubbish. He then arranged to see a careers bloke in the Reading careers office that was next door to the Great Western Hotel in Reading town.

He told the careers bloke that he fancied a job as a typewriter mechanic. I mean, what's better than riding a motorbike? Chatting with the young girls while you repaired their typewriters! He was given another interview with a person at Reids Typewriter shop in the market place. Once more he dressed in a spotlessly clean white shirt, grey flannel trousers and a posh tie. But the ink splattered jacket remained. He entered the shop and told the lady behind the counter that he was there for an interview. He was ushered into a room at the rear of the shop where a formidable respectable lady told him to sit down in front of her desk. She squinted at him through her glasses and asked, "Why do you want to be a typewriter mechanic?" He squirmed in his seat and mumbled a derogatory answer. "I heard from my mate that it was a good job." The answer did not appear to impress her. She leaned forward in her chair and spoke in an officious voice: "Is your mate a typewriter mechanic?" James replied lamely, "No he has only just left school." She smiled and in a friendlier tone spoke again, "Well, young man, if we employ you, you will be doing various tasks about the shop until you are 18 years old. Then you will have to complete your two years army conscription. When you come out of the army we will train you to become a typewriter mechanic."

With the interview concluded he made his way home in low spirits. He sat in the big armchair by the front room window staring gloomily out at the street, when the next-door neighbour walked through the garden gate and knocked on the front door. Reggie B used to pop in occasionally to chat with his uncle Sid, who was his mother's 51-year-old brother. Reggie B was an engine driver based at Reading GWR locomotive depot. He was about 58 years old with a lined face and sharp blue eyes, a self-rolled cigarette dangled from his lips.

Reggie looked at the young lad sitting by the window and spoke. "Got yourself a job yet Jimmy boy?" he said. "No Mr B but I have had an interview," replied the lad trying to make it sound important. Reggie spoke again: "You come with me lad I will get you a job," he said. The young lad looked at him in surprise, "Can you do that Mr B?" asked the lad in reply. "Yes, I will be going to work in an hour's time so be ready and come with me," said Reggie.

Come time for Reggie to go to work, the young lad now had his ramshackle bike ready to follow Reggie along the Oxford Road to Great Knollys Street. Here they turned left and rode across the recreation ground to the large black metal gates that were the entrance to the GWR locomotive depot. Following Reggie through the small pedestrian gate to the left of the main gate, they walked under a bridge and up a slight slope to the shed rail crossing. Walking across the rails they approached a man wearing a bowler hat and a long black rubber type rain coat. The lad noticed that the man was about 50 years of age and had about two days of beard stubble on his face, but he had an air of authority about him. This man was the shed foreman Vic Smith.

Reggie greeted the foreman with a grin on his face saying, "Hey Vic any chance of giving this lad a job?" He pointed at the boy. The foreman looked at the lad with a quizzical look on his face and replied, "Yes, Reg. Take him across to the office and see the clerk." Reg nodded and said thanks then turning to his left he said to the boy, "Hang about here while I put my bike away and lean your old wreck against the shed wall." With that he walked off to the bike shed. The lad leaned his bike against the shed wall and when Reg sauntered back, began to follow him across the nine rail lines and pits at the front of the large engine shed. The lad looked in some awe at the large steam locomotives that were being prepared at the front of the shed. Some were tank engines with the numbers 6100 etc. on the front and some were larger engines with name plates on the side as well as numbers on the front but all were belching columns of black smoke and steam. The loud noise and the smell of coal smoke and engine oil was slightly alarming.

Eventually they arrived at a series of dark brown wooden doors, Reg knocked loudly on a door to the left and when a flap opened a voice said aggressively "What do you want?" This was Len Saunders one of the shed foremen. "This lad wants to see the clerk about a job," said Reg. With that Len opened the door and ushered the lad to the rear of the office block to the clerk's office. Opening the door Len said to the clerk "Sign this lad up for a cleaner's job, please Sid." The clerk was a smart looking chap in a dark suit and wearing a yellow dicky bow tie. He wore rimmed spectacles and was about 50 years old. He sat at his desk and gestured the lad to enter and sit down on a seat opposite his desk. From a drawer in his desk he produced a paper form and handed it to the lad. "Fill this in son," he said. The lad picked up a pen from the desk and wrote on the form nervously. After signing the form, he handed it to the clerk who read it carefully, the clerk then said: "Right son, next week you will be getting a train pass for Swindon with instructions to get to Park House where you will have a medical." With that said he showed the lad out of the office and bid him goodbye. Walking quickly across the lines in front of the shed and hoping he would not be run over by the large noisy steam engines he jumped on his ramshackle bike and rode home with a feeling of success for future lucrative employment his mission accomplished.

SWINDON

The time waiting for the railway pass and instructions seemed endless. The lad whose name on the instruction letter was James Briggs, lived in a council house at 20 Ripley Road. His neighbour was Reggie Bridcutt the engine driver who helped him to get employment with British rail, the 15 years that James had lived here had not made him a fan of Reg. In fact Reg thought him a bloody noisy nuisance and James thought Reg to be a miserable old sod. But for some reason Reg helped him find employment anyway.

Eventually the letter arrived on Monday morning. "There is a letter for you in the front room," said his mother as she rapped on his bedroom door loudly, to arouse him from a deep sleep. With a somewhat grudging reluctance he dragged himself from the warm confines of his bed. Throwing back the covers he fumbled for his clothes and hastily made his way to the location of the important letter. He tore open the envelope and with a feeling of elation read the instructions and also noted the railway pass contained in the envelope. "Bloody good ain't it mum," he shouted to his mother, who was in the kitchen making a welcome pot of hot tea. She brought him a cup of tea and glancing at the letter said: "You will have to get up early tomorrow morning then, won't you?" He looked again at the date and time contained in the instructions. Bloody hell he thought, tomorrow was the date for his important journey to Swindon and he realised that getting up early in the morning was never his strong point. His uncle Sid who lived with them used to say, "You will never be able to get a job because you can't get up in the morning." Well, I will have to prove him wrong, he thought. The day passed too slowly for his liking and an early night to bed he thought would be a good idea. So, at 10pm he retired to his bedroom at the back of the house on the ground floor. The room was actually a second reception room but due to his two brothers taking over his old bedroom upstairs he had moved into the room and made it his own private quarters. Next morning to his surprise he managed to wake at 7am. Hastily getting dressed in some clean crisp white shirt and grey school trousers he managed to knot a somewhat creased tie around his collar. Then, looking in the mirror and combing his dark brylcreemed hair, he was satisfied he looked reasonably tidy. Donning his old school jacket, that was a light-coloured type bomber coat covered in school ink stains. (Caused by fooling about at school obviously). He made his way to the bus stop in Oxford Road. A trolley bus arrived at the stop and he stepped aboard. He then paid the conductor the fare money and sat staring out the window at the early morning traffic.

Arriving at the Broad Street stop he got off, and walked along the road to the Reading station forecourt. Here he showed his pass to the ticket inspector on duty and walked onto platform 3. He noted that there was only a few people on the platform. One of the people standing about waiting for the train he spotted was a boy of his own age. He stood about five foot six tall, same height as himself. But the boy's stature was more robust. He had a light coloured spikey hair style and blue eyes. Looking at James for a while he stepped towards him and said: "Hello mate. Are you going to Swindon for a medical, you know for a job with the railway?"

"Yes, mate that's right, are you going there as well?" replied James.

" Yes, we can go together can't we. By the way my name is Jimmy, Jimmy Ball that is."

James smiled and said, "My names Jimmy as well, Jimmy Briggs."

They both laughed. Just then the Swindon train rolled into the station coming to a halt with a squeal of the brakes. They opened a carriage door and climbed aboard. As they settled down into the third class compartment the train began to move out of the station. They both stared out of the window, watching the West Reading signal box slide out of view as the train gathered speed. Next the Reading locomotive depot came into view. They both watched it also as it slid out of view with the train gathering speed and the sound of the steam engine up front barking loudly.

The journey to Swindon did not take long and soon they were stepping of the train and exiting Swindon station. Both reading their instructions letters they found the way to Park House where they had a rudimentary medical, a colour blindness test and a small writing test. After the medical and tests they were allocated their railway uniforms which consisted of two pair of overalls, one small jacket, one overcoat, one black rubber rain coat and a peaked shiny cap complete with a British Rail badge. Stuffing these garments into a large plastic bag they vacated Park House and made their way back to the station. Arriving at the station Jimmy Ball suggested they go to the cafeteria and buy themselves cups of tea and doughnuts. They sat and waited for the Reading train to arrive, eating and drinking to while away the time. Eventually the train arrived and the journey back to Reading seemed to go quite fast. At the station, they parted company and James, after catching a trolleybus in Broad Street, arrived home at five pm. He threw his bag of British Rail uniform into his bedroom and then climbed into a big comfy chair in the front room and fell asleep. Two days later he received a letter to inform him to report at 6am, on Monday, to Reading loco depot. James wisely went and purchased a large alarm clock with the words of his uncle Sid echoing in his mind. You will never get a job because you can't get up in the morning. Looking at the clock he thought with this noisy big bugger, I will not only wake myself up, but the whole street as well. On Sunday evening he retired to bed early at 10pm. Trying to drift off to sleep he wondered what the next day would be like. Thoughts of the large dark engine shed with its noise and smoke raced through his mind, but then all thoughts stopped as he drifted into a deep sleep.

FIRST BIG DAY AT WORK

A loud clanging noise echoed about the darkened room. A figure stirred slowly in the rumpled bed, and then an arm shot out to smack the alarm clock into silence. A tousled head emerged from the warm bedclothes followed by a body that swung its legs out of the bed and onto the cold linoleum floor. James shook his head to clear the sleepy fog that shrouded his mind, then a shiver ran up his body as he realised how bloody cold that linoleum was to his feet. He heaved himself up from the bed and began to dress. First, he donned his vest and pants followed by a blue denim shirt and denim working jeans. He then put on his blue overall trousers followed by the same coloured overall jacket. He pulled on a thick pair of grey woollen socks that reached up to his knees. Fumbling between his feet he pulled a pair of heavy hob nailed ex-army boots out from under the bed. He put them on and tied the laces tight. Standing up he looked at himself in the small round bedroom mirror. Yep, he thought, looks OK. Actually, looks adult he surmised. Walking to the kitchen he lit the gas stove and placed a full kettle of water on the flame. The water soon boiled and a pot of very hot, strong tea, was soon carried to the living room, with two large cups accompanying it. James then turned on the electric light and small radio. The sounds of the American forces network filled the room. The song was a country and western number, *Railroad steamboat river and canal, some sucker has stolen my gal*. The singer sang sadly. Walking back out of the room James climbed the stairs to his uncle Sid's bedroom. Shaking his uncle gently by the shoulder he whispered: "Come on Sid wakey wakey, tea's made, times five o'clock."

Sid stirred and opened his eyes with disbelief. James up before him, miracles must be real he thought. Entering the living room Sid muttered: "Turn that racket off Jim, it's too early for that."

The song had now changed to a Jim Reeves number. *Put your sweet lips a little closer to the phone, and we can pretend we are together all alone.*

James stifled a laugh and replied: "Aw Sid, don't be mean they're playing our song."

"Turn it off you daft bugger," retorted Sid, grinning at the sounds emanating from the radio and thinking of his nephew's smart reply. After drinking their tea they collected their lunch packs from the kitchen and vacated the house to begin their day's work. Sid was going to the Simmonds brewery where he worked in the malt house. James, with some nervousness, was cycling along the Oxford Road then into Bedford Road and into Great Knollys Street. He cycled across the recreation ground to the large black gates of the loco shed. Pushing his bike through the small side gate he walked under the railway bridge and into the loco shed confines. Placing his bike in the bike shed he then traversed the nine lines and pits to the office block. Again he looked in some awe at the large noisy steam engines that stood in front of the shed being prepared for their day's work. The noise of steam blowers being used to assist combustion on the engines pushed the black smoke out of the chimneys with a noisy blast. A hiss of steam from the engines cylinders as the engines were moved towards the water columns, the sound of metal against metal as the firemen built their fires up, the shouts of commands as the drivers began to move their engines toward the outgoing signal positions.

Compared to the sheltered school life he had just come from, all this seemed unreal. "I am now an adult," he thought. "And now's a good time to start earning loads of dosh."

With this in mind he approached the foreman's office door and tapped on the small shutter. The shutter opened and a face wearing a trilby hat stared out at him. "What?" was the terse inquiry spoken by the face.

"I am reporting for work,' said James. "I am supposed to be starting work as an engine cleaner," he added.

"Alright lad, stay where you are and someone will collect you," replied the face, and with a bang the shutter was closed.

A moment later a rotund figure appeared walking toward him. A man aged about fifty with a bald head and wearing thick spectacles looked at him and asked: "You Mr Briggs the new cleaner?"

"Yes sir" replied James. "That's me"

"Right Mr Briggs let's get you booked in. By the way, I am Mr Burt your chargehand."

They shook hands and James was then led to another smart office window on the opposite wall. Mr Burt tapped on the window and a face appeared.

"Book this lad in will you Sid, his name is Mr Briggs, a new cleaner. OK?"

Mr Burt turned to face James and said "Sid will book you in and explain what you are to do. OK?"

James stood facing the small window and soon a face appeared again and said: "Right Mr Briggs this is your pay check, take note of its number and don't bloody lose it."

A small oval metal disc was pushed out of the window in front of him and he noted the number printed on it, 365.

"Now," continued the person behind the window. "Every day you book on give your name and pay check number to the booking-on clerk, he will then give you the check and book you on duty. At the end of your shift, hand in your pay check before you go home." With that said the window closed.

Mr Burt gestured James to follow him as he turned to walk further into the shed confines. They walked about 50 yards until they faced a large dark wooden door to their right. Pushing open the big door Mr Burt nodded at James to enter. Stepping into the room he was slightly awed at the scene before him. The room measured about 12-foot square with a long wooden bench to the right-hand wall, with a long wooden table in front of it. Another long bench was on the opposite side of the table. On the wall by the door was another bench same pattern as the other two. In front of him was a four-foot large window frame, with a series of small glass panes. Most of the glass panes were either missing or cracked. To the right of the window was a large Belfast type china sink on bricks, with one cold water tap. In the centre of the room was a large metal stove glowing red hot. Around the stove was a circular metal tray filled with ash and other debris, namely old cigarette packets, food wrappers, drink cans and cigarette stubs, some spilling onto the floor area. Sitting around the room on the benches were about nine young lads dressed in overalls and wearing engine oil caps.

Most of the lads were smoking and a haze of smoke filled the room. He noted that the walls were made of brick and were painted black up to a height of about eight feet, the rest of the wall was made of wooden planking painted yellow and reached up to the roof high above.

A familiar face suddenly appeared before him, it was Georgie Goodal, his old mate from his junior school days at Grovelands.

"Whatcha mate. Ain't seen you for a while. How's it hanging?" George asked with a broad grin on his face.

"Hiya George, great to see you again," replied James with a returned grin. Another lad stood up and James recognised him as Jimmy Ball his companion from the Swindon trip.

"Like a cup of tea mate," asked Jimmy.

"Thanks, could do with one mate," replied James and with the greetings over they sat and chatted over old times and about school days. The time chatting and generally goofing about passed quickly and James noted the time on his watch was about 7.30. He thought blimey we booked on duty at 6am and its now 7.30. When are we supposed to begin work? As he was thinking this the cabin door suddenly burst open and a voice shouted: "Come on you lazy buggers. There is work to be done."

Standing in the doorway was Mr Burt who with a gesture of "follow me", began to walk back to his office expecting the lads too follow him. Everybody filed out of the room and walked to Mr Burt's office. James said to George: "What's Mr Burt like as a boss, George mate?" he asked.

"You mean Freddie? We don't call him Mr," replied George. "To us cleaners he is alright. Nice bloke, and remember to call him Freddie, not Mr," said George with a grin.

"You will meet the other charge hand next week because he is on night shifts at the moment, his name is Charlie Steen and he a good bloke as well."

Upon entering the room James noted several bass brooms and large shovels propped against the wall, also arranged on the floor were two buckets filled with oil, and cotton waste. There was also a large ball of dry cotton waste next to the buckets. Several of the cleaners picked up the brooms and shovels and walked out of the room. The rest of the cleaners listened while Freddie Burt gave them instructions. "You will be cleaning 6102. It's standing on line two. OK?" he said. "Right. Off you go, and clean it well," he added. "What's the brooms and shovels for," inquired James speaking to George. "Oh, you will find out later," said George not imparting any more information.

Collecting the buckets of oil and dry cotton waste the cleaners walked out of Freddie's office. They located the engine 6102 on number two shed line. The steam engine was a prairie tank locomotive. To James it appeared large as he stood next to its wheels and connecting rods.

"Right, Jim, this is what you must do," said George with a smile on his face. Pointing to the front of the engine he said: "See that big round door on the front there, well you have to get up there and open it." James climbed up onto the front of the engine, and after turning the large door handles to unlock it he pulled the door open. George had now climbed up beside him and said: "Climb inside and look up into the corner of the chimney, there you will see a lever that must be pulled."

James, with some hesitation, climbed into the confines of the smoke box and looked up into the chimney. Soot and cinders were falling down the neck of his shirt, as he struggled to find the lever, with a loud clang the smoke box door suddenly shut, and he was engulfed in darkness.

"Fuck you George, open the bloody door," he shouted, but the door remained closed for several minutes with the sounds of laughter coming down the chimney.

After several minutes, the door opened and a grinning face appeared: "Got you there mate, didn't I?" said the face.

"Ha ha George. Very funny," responded James. "Now let's be bloody sensible and get this engine cleaned."

Annoyed with being so stupid to fall for such a trick James volunteered to clean the smoke box area, climbing up high onto the handrail at the side of the smoke box, he applied the thick oil on to the metal surface. After rubbing it all over the surface, he polished it off with the clean cotton waste. He stood back to admire his handiwork. The smoke box and chimney surface shone black. Nice job thought James. He had cleaned along the rest of the boiler surface as well, so all parts gleamed much brighter. George came and stood beside him and, looking up at the chimney, said: "You ain't finished yet mate. You got to brickdust the copper top and safety valve cover."

George handed him a tin of orange coloured ground up brickdust and moist cotton waste. George climbed up onto the engine with him, and the both of them sitting high up on the smoke box, rubbed the brick dust into the copper band around the chimney top. The copper began to shine brightly and with this finished they rubbed the rest of the brick dust into the brass safety valve cover until this also shone like new. Climbing back onto the ground, they stood and admired their handiwork. The rest of the cleaner lads came round to stand with them. Being satisfied that the prairie tank steam engine now looked fine, they all decided it was time for another tea break.

James looked at his watch, the time showed nine o'clock. Blimey, he thought, we have only been out of the cabin for an hour and half and we are going back in again. They trooped back into the cleaners' cabin and all took out their tea cans. They then went into the drivers' cabin next door, where a huge kettle that sat on a gas ring continuously boiled. Returning to the cleaners' cabin George began to point out the various cleaners to James. The names George imparted as he pointed too each cleaner were, Tony Beasley, a tallish chap with dark hair, Bob Brazelle, tall with fair hair, Brian Stratton, slim chap with a bit of teenage acne. Terry Wiltshire, tall lad with protruding teeth, Ken Dodd came to James' mind with a chuckle. Ray Atree, a tall lad with fair hair, Ray Carter, big stocky chap with pleasant features, Kenny Wotton with a big mop of fair hair and girly good looks and then Dave Hemmings, dark haired fellow who called everybody cobber. Just then two more cleaners entered the cabin, George said the two just coming in were Rod Fuller, another tallish chap with curly hair and wide grin James noted, and "Bill Wyatt. We call him Lofty."

James could see why, as lofty Wyatt was a very tall gangly youth, taller than the rest of them. Jimmy Ball of course James had already met. With all names now made known, they sat and drank their over-sweet hot tea. The time went by quickly and soon it was 10. 15. Like earlier it seemed the breaks being taken were rather long, thought James, but Freddie Burt did not seem concerned.

At 10. 20 the cleaners reluctantly filed out of the cabin and headed for Freddie's office. Arriving at the office they were again issued with buckets and oil.
"Number 6923 Croxteth hall on number 3 bay. Right. Off you go," ordered Freddie.
Carrying the buckets of oil and cotton waste they made their way to number three bay.
Standing there was a steam engine much larger than the previous one they had cleaned.
"Right," said George. "You Jimmy boy will be cleaning hard side boiler."
James looked perplexed. "What the devil is hard side boiler," he enquired.
George pointed up to the boiler side and said: "See that bloody great big pipe running along the side of the boiler? Well that's called hard side boiler, because you have got to clean that as well."
James climbed up onto the large Hall class engine and commenced cleaning the hard side boiler with a good feeling. He now began to feel part of the cleaning team.

Tools were laid down at 12 o'clock and the cleaners once again filed back to their mess room. Tea made and sandwiches being consumed they stayed there until One o'clock. Refreshed, they returned to the now shiny 6923 Croxteth Hall engine, and after giving it a cursory polish, they stopped work at 1.30. After getting a bucket of hot water from Freddie's office (he kept a bucket of hot water constantly on the top of his stove for this purpose) they washed and then the shout went up: "INITIATION!"
All eyes were on James, and a chant went up, everybody singing: "SING SING OR SHOW YOUR RING,"
This went on for several minutes getting louder and louder. James was alarmed, he could never sing a note and only pretended to sing at school, silently moving his lips to the music. He also did not know the words to any song. An idea came into his head. He thought I will sing the *Happy Wanderer* but in German. They will not understand the language so I can make up the words. James had attempted to learn a smattering of German while at school, but learned most of it from an American army guide supplied to the army forces in Europe. James reluctantly climbed onto the tabletop and began to sing loudly, while lumps of cotton waste and other debris were thrown at him. "Ich liebe to gain ien vandering, langs der bergen sperg."
He continued his voice getting louder. "Ich liebe to gain ien vandering mit mien napsak on mien back,"
"TRA laa lee, trala lee, mit mien napsak on mien back."
He repeated the song once again and then climbed down from the table. He grinned at his motley audience. But they announced the initiation was not complete yet. This said, four pairs of hand grabbed hold of him and lifted him back onto the table. Laying him prostrate on his back they undid his trousers and rubbed handfuls of fire ash into his family jewels. Initiation complete they then went of to the shed office and booked off duty. James rode his bike home feeling

at peace with himself; glad that his first day at work had gone so well. Little did he know that things would take a turn for the worse.

RAGE

The next week James was getting familiar with the cleaning routine and was gaining some speed in his cleaning mode. On the Monday morning after he had completed his part of the engine, he decided to make an early cup of tea. Walking to the cleaners' cabin, he entered to see a tall person standing by the window area at the rear of the room. The person wore a black rubberised raincoat that reached to well below his knees. He wore a peaked British Rail cap pulled low over his forehead.
He glared at James as he entered the cabin. With a gruff grunt he spoke: "Got a fag mate?"
James answered: "Sorry mate, I don't smoke." With that said the person hawked up a mouthful of green phlegm and spat it at James. With disgusted astonishment James saw the vile gob of phlegm hit his right leg. It hung there like a slimy green ball.
The person spoke again: "I said have you got a fag mate?"
James again answered: "No. I told you, I don't smoke." The person again hawked up another mouthful of green phlegm, and spat it at James.
This time it hit his left leg, and hung there like before. A sudden intense incandescent rage entered James' senses. He made a lunge at this disgusting person grabbing his right hand, and with both of his own hands he twisted the limb violently outwards. The person with a sharp gasp collapsed onto the ash-ridden floor. James jumped astride the prone body. Sitting on his chest he pinned the person's arms to the floor with his knees. James then crossed his own wrists and grabbing two handfuls of the persons shirt collar, pushed his knuckles into his neck, below his ears. Leaning forward with his nine and a half stone weight he muttered to the body below him.
"I am now going to finish you off you bastard,"
As he was saying this two cleaners entered the cabin and seeing the two bodies grappling on the floor exclaimed: "What the fuck's happening here?"
Two pairs of hands grabbed James by the arms and pulled him upright.
The other person staggered to his feet and rubbing his neck said out loud: ""You're fucking mad, you are."
He then staggered to the wooden bench and sitting down leaned forward with his head in his hands.
"You alright mate?" enquired one of the cleaners who had come to his rescue.
"Yeah, but he is fucking mad," he repeated glaring at James.
Tony Beasley and Terry Wiltshire who were the two cleaners, asked James "What happened mate?"
"You don't want to know," replied James "It was bloody disgusting," he added.
The incident over, tea was made and things carried on as normal. He had learned it from a self-defence book. What James did not realise was that the strangle hold he used was a grip that the mafia used to kill their opponents.

THE RAT.

September. The weather was getting colder and the mornings darker. He was now getting used to rising early in the mornings. He still made his uncle's tea and woke him with a chuckle. At work as he got used to the cleaning routine, he tried to learn more about the steam engines' mechanical make up. This was to be short-lived. Arriving at work one morning himself, and another cleaner Bob Brazelle were summoned to Freddie's office. Worrying that he was going to get in trouble about the earlier fighting incident, he entered the office.
Freddie looked up at them from his office chair. "Are you two interested in making a bit more money?" he asked.
Bob looked surprised, and nodding at James said: "Of course we are Fred."
Freddie continued: "Well, the company can't employ anybody to do shed labouring. So, if you two would like to clean the shed tops and pits, keep the shed tidy, they will pay you an adult wage."
James sighed with relief. He was pleased that no mention was made of the fight, and delighted at the idea of earning more money. Freddie, rising from his chair, took them outside of his office. He pointed at two large bass brooms and two large shovels leaning against an even larger wooden wheelbarrow. "There are your tools, look after them and do a good job," he said.
He then disappeared into his office leaving the two cleaners to arrange how they were to manage the task. Starting one each end of the shed they worked towards each other, leaving small piles of debris to be picked up later. At nine o'clock they stopped work and went into the cabin for a tea break. While they were sitting sipping their hot sweet tea, the figure of Terry Wiltshire appeared through the doorway. In his outstretched hands he carried a big brown dead rat. With a wide toothy grin he said: "Look what I've got."
James and Bob looked at him with some revulsion. "It's a bloody rat, horrible thing," said Bob.
With a proud voice Terry replied: "Yea, but ain't it great, look at it, not a mark on it." He shoved the rat towards them.
"What the hell are you going to do with a dead stinking rat?" enquired James. He stepped back away from the vile object that was being shoved towards him.
Terry said with another toothy grin "We can have some fun with it." He stroked the rat as though it was a cherished pet. "We can put it in somebody's jacket pocket," he said.
"It's too big for that you twit," said Bob.
A look of concern came over Terry's face. "Well, we can shove it up the sleeve," he muttered.
So, the plan agreed, he went over to the clothes pegs and selected a jacket. Taking the rat, he gently pushed it into the jacket's sleeve. He then carefully replaced the jacket on its peg. The deed complete they sat down on the benches and waited to see who the lucky owner of the jacket was. The cleaners who were booking off duty at two o'clock began entering the cabin. After washing their hands at the sink they began to select their jackets from the pegs.

The guilty miscreants watched in silence as Terry Forrester walked over to the pegs and selected the jacket. He pushed his arms into the sleeves, frowning at the odd weight of the jacket, and the rat suddenly shot out and landed with a splat on the floor. With a loud terrified scream, Terry ran across the floor and in abject terror, jumped up onto the bench and tried to claw his way through the wall. The cabin was filled with loud laughter as the guilty parties watched poor Terry climb down off the bench.

Looking down at the dead rat, and gaining some composure, he grinned and said in a loud voice, "You rotten bastards, I nearly shit myself."
The other lads clapped Terry on the back and smiling said what a good sport he was. But Mr Wiltshire had another plan forming in his mind. What else could he do with this rat?
He picked up the rat from the floor and looking around selected a tea can from the table. He then removed the cap and shoved the rat into the can with the head showing over the lip. He replaced the cap and put the tea can back on the table.
"Can't believe you just did that," said Bob.
Terry stood back and looking at Bob said, "It's only a joke mate," Bob did not look impressed. "Somebody has got to drink from that can, it's not nice," Bob protested. Little did James know it would be himself.

The other cleaners began to enter the cabin and it was poor old George Goodal who picked up the tea can. Intending to make a nice can of sweet tea. He frowned as he noticed the can was heavier than normal. He removed the cap and seeing the dead rat he exclaimed in a loud voice. "What rotten fuckers done this?"
There was no laughter this time.
"James spoke saying in an apologetic tone: "Sorry mate we should not have done it."
Taking the can from George he walked out of the cabin and tipped the dead rat into the inspection pit. He returned and gave the can back to George saying "Give it a good clean mate, it should be ok."
George accepted the can and he then had to share James' tea can for the rest of the shift. Next day George walked into the cleaners' cabin and announced that his can had been thoroughly cleaned with bleach and disinfectant. He then said to James: "Will you have a cup of tea with me mate?"
James without hesitation said "Yes George. Of course I will."
But hoped that George had cleaned the can as he said. No harm came to either of them, so dead rat or not, they used the can all day.

THE BULLY

The work in the shed began to earn James a lot of money. Some times he was taking home more money than his father. His shoebox was filling nicely with pound notes. Working long hours and enjoying the comradeship he felt very secure. The older cleaners were being promoted and new ones employed. Brian Melhuish started working with them. Brian was a lad about 5 foot four, not very tall but with a great sense of humour. Raymond Atree had also starting work with them. A tall lad with a quiet nature and a ready smile.

One morning while all sitting having their nine o'clock tea break another new cleaner walked into the cabin. He was tallish with brown curly hair. He wore a brown army sweater under his overalls. He introduced himself to the cleaners as Brian Maggs. Brian was 23 years old and was always boasting about his time in the army. He had served in Malaya he said, and attacked rebel communist forces in the jungle there. Soon he had the young lads listening to his boasts and running around obeying his demands. Go make my tea. Give me a fag. Go to the shops and get me a can of coke. These demands became common. One morning James sat quietly drinking his tea and eating a cheese and pickle sandwich. The cabin began to fill with the other cleaners. Brian Maggs sat opposite James with Kenny Wotton, both chatting together.
Brian stared at James and with a loud voice said: "Hey you there, go and make my tea, will you."
James looked at the bully and in a nervous voice replied: "Go make your own bloody tea. I'm not your servant."
A silence filled the cabin, then a whoooooops sound echoed round the room as the cleaners acknowledged his refusal. Brian stood up and glaring at his defiant victim growled. "Right you little sod I will sort you out later."
James replied in a shaky nervous voice. "You lay a bloody hand on me and I will make sure you lose your job, or fall on your arse."
The bully said again: "I will bloody sort you out later smart arse."
With that said the tea break carried on as normal. Tea break over, the cleaners filed out of the cabin to their places of work. James stayed in the cabin until last. Hoping that Brian would leave him alone. He walked out of the cabin to where he had left his tools. As he walked to the front of the shed he saw the bully and a bunch of cleaners standing next to a prairie tank engine. They had their buckets of oil and cotton waste and were about to start cleaning the engine. As he went to walk by them, Brian strode towards him. The sound of the song by Nat King Cole filled James' mind - *There may be trouble ahead, but while there's moonlight and dancing, love and romance, lets face the music and dance!*
Brian stared at him and in an aggressive voice snarled "Ok Mr Toughie, let's see what you can do."
He loomed over James in a threatening manner, smirking at his small frame. Bugger thought James I have got to do something, so he reached up and with his hand grabbed hold of Brian's right shirt collar. With his left hand he grabbed hold of his right overall sleeve. Then kneeling down he pulled Brian over his knee. With a strangled cry the bully fell heavily to the ground, hitting his head on the concrete. He cried out in a shocked voice "Fuck me he did it!" The other cleaners were laughing with delight. Turning his back on the embarrassed bully, James

continued to his place of work, cleaning the shed tops. A smile on his face he could not believe what had just happened. That self defence book I bought, he thought, the moves really work. After this incident Brian did not continue with his bullying and ceased to work as a cleaner. What happened to him James did not know or care.

THE FLAT BUCKET

Part of the shed labouring work in the winter consisted of looking after the frost fires. These were braziers placed close to the water columns to prevent them from freezing. The columns were located in the loco shed but also in Reading station and the west junction shunting yard. Going around with a heavy four-wheeled trolley loaded with coal, James and Bob fuelled the frost fires in Reading station. When this was complete, the trolley was abandoned and a long trek to the west Reading shunting yard was made. The shunting yard was by Little Johns Lane. When they reached the yard they found that there was only a small amount of coal available. James and Bob watched as a goods train came slowly up the goods line towards them.
Shouting up at the fireman they asked: "Can you chuck us some coal down mate?"
The response was not encouraging. "Fuck off!" was the terse reply.
"You mean sod! Chuck us some coal down mate," shouted back Bob.
With that several large lumps of coal were heaved their way, narrowly missing them both. The fireman laughed as he hurled several more lumps of coal their way. "Bloody retard" muttered James but at least they now had enough coal to keep the frost fire ablaze.

Returning to the loco depot they went around the depot and filled the frost fire braziers to the brim. That should last for a while they agreed. Looking at their watches, they saw the time was six o'clock. The shift had lasted 12 hours. More pound notes for the shoebox thought James with a smile. After washing the coal dust and grime from their hands and faces, they both wearily made their way home. Another day to begin at six o'clock next morning.

Next day Freddie gave them a break from shed labouring. He put them back on the engine cleaning gang. The first engine to clean was a Hall class locomotive situated on number six bay. Collecting the buckets of oil and cotton waste the cleaners arrived at the place of work. The buckets of oil placed on the ground, they began to decide who was to clean what areas of the engine. James was chatting to Ray Atree.

Talking about the latest films in the cinemas in Reading. "*Shane* is a good film, on next week at the Rex," said James as he leaned forward to pull a wad of oily waste from the tin bucket.
As he bent down a hand grabbed him by the shoulder and heaved him violently backward. "What the ****!" the words stopped short as a large set of wheels and side rods narrowly missed his head. The bucket he was about to use, with a metallic crunch was squashed flat under the front wheels of the engine. It was a

Hall class engine that had came through the shed from the turntable area. But the driver had not sounded the whistle. This was a requirement when entering the shed confines from the turntable.

The driver was on the opposite side of the engine and failed to see the cleaners. Hearing the crunch of the flat bucket, he stopped the engine, and leaning over the side cried out: "What the fuck are you lot up to?" not realising how close he had been to flattening James.

The lads shouted back to the driver "Sound your bloody whistle mate."
The driver with a stern look on his face continued through the shed and the cleaners continued with their tasks. Minutes later Charley Steen the cleaners' charge hand, came hurriedly towards them. The driver evidently made a complaint.
"What the devil have you lot been up to now?" he asked shaking his grey haired head in worry.
"Nothing Charley, everything is fine," said Ray.
Satisfied nobody was harmed Charley retreated to his office. James could not thank Ray enough. If he had not pulled him back he shuddered at the thought of what may have happened. Locomotive sheds are dangerous areas he reminded himself. He had not heard the engines approach, not at all. Be more alert he reminded himself again. Be alert!

SLOUGH ACCIDENT.

The early morning began as normal; it was a damp September day. The cold air chilled James as he rode his old ramshackle bike along the Oxford Road. The morning was dark and the sky threatened rain with heavy clouds blotting out any moonlight. At 5.30am he did not expect the waning moon to provide much light but without any lights on his bike it might have dispelled his guilt a bit. He plodded on towards Norcot junction roundabout when to his alarm he noticed another bicycle heading towards him from the right hand side of the roundabout. Sat upright on this bicycle was the figure of a policeman. "Fuck it, just my bloody luck. Now I am going to get a good bollocking and a fine." The tall helmeted figure pulled across the road and came alongside of him.
He spoke: "Good morning lad. Early start is it?"
James reasoned the officer must have noticed his peaked cap with the badge of British Railways across it.
"Er um yea. Too early," muttered the perturbed young railwayman.
"Weather's not too good either is it?" said the constable.
"No might even rain," lamented James, when suddenly the constable said with surprise.
"You cheeky young sod. You haven't got any lights!"
James was now in trouble, he tried to think of a sensible reply but only managed to say: "Sorry about that mate, I didn't think it would be so dark."
They were now cycling past Grovelands School, and as the policeman pulled across the right hand side of the road, where a police telephone box was situated. He said: "If you see another constable on your way, do not tell him you saw me. OK?" and he was gone.

Bloody hell, thought James, I got away with that. He then pedalled furiously the rest of the way to Great Knollys Street before his luck changed. He booked on duty and headed to the cleaners' cabin. The night crew were preparing to go home. As he entered the cabin he noticed it was slightly chillier than normal. He also noticed there was even fewer glass panes in the large window.

"Where's the glass panes gone?" he asked with curiosity.

"Ha ha," replied Brian Stratton, a fair-haired cleaner. "Last night we went up the station and collected a number of cups and saucers that had been left on the platform benches."

"Well what's the glass panes got to do with that?" queried James.

"We got bored so we chucked 'em out the bloody window and broke more panes" chuckled Brian. "If you look out the window it ain't 'alf a mess," he added.

James sighed. These cleaners are something else. The phrase "You couldn't make it up" entered his mind.

The morning's cleaning and shed labouring carried on as normal until 10am. Just as the cleaners were finishing their breakfast break Freddie Burt pushed open the big wooden door and announced with a concerned edge to his voice, "I want half a dozen volunteers!"

He surveyed the suspicious faces in silence. "What are we volunteering for? Asked Bob Brazelle a tall fair headed cleaner.

Freddie with a disturbed intonation to his voice said: "There is a 6100 Prairie tank on number six outside pit, and it's a bit of a mess!"

The curious expectant faces stared at him and someone asked "What sort of mess Fred?"

Freddie took a deep breath and replied with a sigh of distress, "It ran over a platelayer at Slough and the remains of his body, poor chap, is spread all over the engine, and the drivers are refusing to prepare the engine until all of it is cleaned off!"

He looked at the faces that were now showing revulsion, and in an imploring voice asked: "Well lads who are volunteering?"

George Goodal nudged James and whispered "Shall we do it mate? Freddie might give us a longer tea break later?"

James reluctantly agreed, and, Bob with several others volunteered as well. They followed Freddie to his office and collected the cleaning materials. When the hesitant volunteers arrived at the site they spotted the Prairie tank standing ominously dark and silent on the pit. Someone had attempted to clean the wheels where scrape marks were evident. The smoke box front was covered in a white fat type residue. James shuddered and tried not to visualise what it could be.

He looked at George and asked warily: "Shall we clean the underneath, the link gear and that?"

George grinned: "Yeah, let's get a couple of buckets to stand on."

He wandered off in search of the buckets with James following. They came back with two buckets taken from the coal stage area engines. Climbing into the pit they crouched under the front of the engine and crawled under the gear link rods and wheel axels. Here they both stood on the buckets to reach the underside of the boiler cover and rods. The sight that reached their eyes was not pleasant. There were globules of fat and hair stuck to the boiler casing and rods. They both began to clean the rods with the oily cotton waste. Rubbing vigorously they were removing the obnoxious residue bit-by-bit trying to ignore its content. When they were satisfied it was clean enough, they tried to clean the underside of the boiler casing. George took out his gas cigarette lighter and tried to ignite some of the residue. James was now feeling slightly nauseous and said: "Stop fucking about mate, let's get this finished and I could do with a good cup of tea."

George laughed and between them they hurriedly completed the cleaning task, in the fervent hope of never having to do so again.

The other cleaners had cleaned the smoke box and buffer plank and the engine now looked clean enough to be prepared for its next task.

Freddie was pleased with their well-administered assignment and had no complaints from the drivers. So they did get a much longer break to quench their need for tea that day. The strange thing was that the episode was never mentioned again.

JACK CLAY

The day started bright and sunny. James and Bob had been rostered to clean the loco shed as usual. Starting their work at 6.30 they made good progress and at 12 o'clock decided to take an much-needed tea break. While sitting in the cabin drinking their tea a young fireman walked in and, in a loud voice, said: "Whatcha mates. How's things?"

James noticed he stood about five foot seven. He had a black spikey haircut and a face that was red with many acne yellow spots. He sat down and said: "Have you any sandwiches you don't need?"

James said: "Yes I have some. Would you like them? They are cheese and pickle."

"Great, I would love them," said the fireman. "By the way my name's Jack Clay."

James took a pack of sandwiches from his bag and, handing them to Jack, said: "Here mate. You're your welcome."

He thought Jack might be hungry and eat the sandwiches, but he laid the wrapped food onto the table and carefully unwrapped them. He then peeled away the top piece of bread to expose the cheese and pickle contents. He hawked up a mouthful of green phlegm and spat it into the sandwich. The disgusting deed completed he carefully wrapped up the food and left it on the table.

Witnessing this gross act repulsed James and Bob. A few minutes later a cleaner entered the cabin. Jack greeted him saying: "Hiya mate. You look hungry, would you like a sandwich?"

The young lad's eyes lit up as he replied: "Yes mate. I am bloody starving. Thanks."

The sandwiches were handed to the lad by Jack who said: "Cheese and pickle mate."

The lad unwrapped the food and consumed it with relish. As he ate the food with a wide grin on his face, he must have wondered why Jack Clay was giggling to himself, and the others were looking so guilty. The incident over James and Bob continued with the shed labouring. At 2 o'clock they were asked to work on until four o'clock. Freddie Burt said the pits on numbers 4, 5,and 6 bays needed cleaning of sludge and shale that had been washed out of the engines boilers. The two of them crawled under the large steam engines. Bent double they shovelled the muck through the engines wheels and onto the tops. They then had to load the muck into the large wheelbarrows and trundle them round to the back of the shed. The sludge made the wheelbarrows very heavy and it took some strength to move them to the point of delivery. Two other cleaners were helping with this task and soon a big pile of ash and sludge was deposited to the rear of the shed. Now the next job was to shovel the debris into a 16-ton wagon. The cleaners, with great youthful energy, completed the task in good time. The day's work over James booked of duty and rode wearily home along the Oxford Road. Arriving home he took off his overalls and, after a good wash, flopped wearily into the big armchair and fell into a deep sleep. This method of work was to be his for the next eight months. He hoped that during this period he would not encounter the odious Jack Clay again. It was not to be.

Several weeks later Freddie asked James and Bob if they would like to work a Saturday overtime shift. They agreed readily, Bob thinking of the extra money for his motorbike and James thought of filling his shoebox faster. The work entailed emptying a 13-ton coal wagon of its load. Then shovelling it into the shed boiler room. They arrived at work 6am. The weather was cold but with the sun shining bright the job seemed, though hard, quite enjoyable. They made their way to the side of the loco shed, where a 13-ton wagon of coal was stopped opposite the boiler room. They hammered the side flap open. It fell with a loud crash with lumps of coal shooting out onto the ground. They began shovelling the coal out of the wagon onto the ground. When they had a good pile on the ground they then shovelled it into the boiler room. They worked hard until 12 o'clock. With all the coal shovelled into the boiler room they went to the cleaners' cabin for a well-earned break. They made a can of tea and as they were sitting relishing the sweet nectar, the cabin door burst open. Standing in the doorway was the figure of Jack Clay. "Whatcha mates," he greeted them.
"What do you want Jack?" enquired Bob, looking at Jack with suspicion.
"I've come to see how you boys are getting along," he said. He sat down and began chatting about general topics related to the loco depot. After a few minutes chatting, Jack stood up. He stood in the middle of the room with his back to the stove. With the stoves side glowing red hot Jack turned around, and undoing his overall trouser buttons, urinated onto the red-hot stove. Stinking clouds of ammonia filled the air as the vile liquid sizzled on the side of the stove. "Bloody hell, you dirty sod!" exclaimed James as he and Bob rushed to exit the cabin. The obnoxious stink followed them out into the shed. The door to the drivers cabin was flung open with the drivers and firemen choking on the fumes, rushing out.
"Which of you little fuckers have done that?" a driver demanded, holding a handkerchief to his nose.
James and Bob protested their innocence as Jack furtively walked by them grinning evilly. The shed foreman Wally Holt, also holding a handkerchief to his nose, marched toward them.
"Jesus wept, what have you buggers been up to now?' he asked
"It wasn't us," said Bob.
"Who was it then?" demanded Wally.
Tommy Neate the other foreman walked toward them saying. "Right you buggers sod of home before you get into any more trouble."
The two of them could not exit the shed quick enough to escape the wrath of the recipients of Jack's evil act.

Luckily to their relief they were not to encounter Jack Clay again.

THE BIG DAY

The Christmas of 1955 arrived and three more cleaners arrived. Several of the present cleaners were promoted to the footplate. The new lads were Vernon Paxford, John Keen, and John Parker. James and Bob were still shed labouring, when they should have been learning about the craft of steam engines. There was one day of tuition in the shed classroom. That was all.

As James was cleaning the area around number six bay, a familiar figure approached him. It was Reggie, his next-door neighbour. Reg tapped James on the shoulder.

"Hello Reg, how are you?" said James.

"Got a little job for you," said Reg.

"I am a little bit busy Reg," responded James.

"It won't take long, and I will give you a stick of chewing gum," said Reg with a grin.

James sighed and said: "Alright Reg what can I do for you? And you can keep your gum mate. Never liked it much."

With a wave Reg motioned James to follow him. They walked to the rear of the shed and Reg pointed to a 9734 tank engine stationed there. He spoke: "Can you oil the motions for me, underneath the engine?"

James looked at the engine and replied: "Yes Reg. Of course I will, but you will have to show me."

Reg climbed up upon the engines footplate and reappeared with a metal bucket. He climbed down from the engine and gave James the bucket; he then removed a large oiling can from the engine's toolbox. Reg handed the oiling can to James.

"Now take the bucket and can underneath the engine," Reg ordered.

James jumped down into the inspection pit and disappeared with a crouching movement underneath the engine. He felt the heat of the firebox above his head and drops of hot water dripped onto his cap. When he got to the motions area he was able to stand upright. Reg, standing to the side of the engine was looking at James as he stood up.

"Stand on the bucket and you will be able to reach the motions oil points," he said.

James scraped the bucket along the pit's concrete base, and stood on it to reach the oiling point. He removed the corks situated on top of the motions and filled the motion gears with oil. Job completed he crawled back out from the engines hot confines. Climbing out of the pit he felt he had learned another lesson. The months seemed to pass to slow now thought James. Himself and Bob were becoming firm friends and spent lot of social time together.

They went to the Rex cinema to see the film *The Blackboard Jungle* with Glenn Ford and the music score of *Rock Around the Clock*, by Bill Haley. Great film, they thought, and brilliant music. The spring weather was nearing with the mornings much lighter. One morning in late April, Freddie told James to go to the clerk's office. He needed to talk to him. James made his way to the clerk's office and knocked nervously on the door. A voice told him to enter. James opened the door and stepped inside, the familiar smell pervaded his nose. The clerk, still dressed in the dark suit and yellow dicky bow, greeted him.

"Come in lad and sit yourself down." The clerk pulled out a sheath of papers and looking at them said: "You won't be 16 until June, but we are short of firemen, so we would like you to book on Monday as fireman on the Coley branch."

James could not believe his luck. No more shed labouring, no more engine cleaning, he was to be promoted to fireman grade.

The clerk spoke again. "Do you know rule 55?" he asked.

James replied: "Yes sir, protection of the train." and he explained what this entailed.

The clerk spoke again: "Do you know how to check the water level when an engine is in steam?"

James replied yes again and explained the procedure.

"That's all then lad, book on Monday at 12 o'clock. Your driver will be Eddie Price. Don't be late."

Floating on air James walked back to the cleaners' cabin. He made a can of tea and sat chatting to the other cleaners enjoying the knowledge that this would be the last time.

THE COLEY BRANCH

Monday morning James relaxed in his bed, not rising until 9 o'clock. Bloody luxury, he thought. Not having to get up at 4.45am. Uncle Sid will be making his own morning tea again he mused. Throwing the warm bedclothes to one side he swung his legs out of the bed. Sitting on the side of the bed he looked at his shoebox that sat in the corner of the room. He noticed with satisfaction that the pile of one pound notes was filling the box nicely. Dressing himself in a blue denim shirt, blue jeans and thick woollen socks, he then pulled on his old ex-army boots. Ready for the fray he thought as he surveyed himself in the bedroom mirror. He walked out of the bedroom into the small kitchen, his boots resounding loudly on the hard flooring. His mother, standing by the sink, smiled at him saying: "Noisy bugger. Do you want a cup of tea and some toast?"

"Thanks Ma that will do nicely," he responded.

Taking his tea to the living room, he sat in the big comfy chair that he usually had a nap in. Eating his toast and sipping his tea he wondered what the day would be like. He worried that he did not really have a clue about the job of firing a steam engine. Well, he thought, it can't be that difficult. The time went by quickly and at 11 o'clock he donned himself in a clean set of overalls. He put on his short serge jacket, and shiny peaked cap complete with the British Railways red badge. Saying goodbye to his mother, he mounted his smart new racing bike and cycled of along the Oxford Road to work. Arriving at the loco depot he booked on duty in the lobby used by the drivers and firemen.

"Book us on Sid," he proudly prompted the booking clerk. "I am on the 12 o'clock Coley today."

That accomplished he waited in the lobby for his driver. Because he had come in so early for his shift, he had to wait sometime before his driver Eddie Price arrived. A stocky chap aged about 60, wearing a cloth cap, walked into the lobby. As he booked on duty James heard him say something about Coley.

"Excuse me, are you the Coley driver?" asked James.

The driver looked at him and tipping back his cloth cap said: "Yes young man, and you are Mr Briggs I take it?"

James looking at the tall burly man replied: "Yes I am your fireman for today.

"Right young man, let's get started. By the way my name is Eddie."

With the curt introductions over, Eddie beckoned James to follow him. They walked through the shed confines and coming to the turntable area continued walking. They passed the coal stage where several engines waited to be cleaned and filled with fresh coal. Crossing the Cow Lane Bridge and walking about half a mile alongside the main line they arrived at the West Reading junction shunting yard. James noted that a small 22 class tender engine was stationed in the yard. Walking over to the dormant engine Eddie grabbed hold of the handrails and climbed aboard. James followed him, and stepping onto the footplate looked around at the tidy work area.

The fireman he was relieving greeted him "Whacha mate. How are you?"

He did not wait for a reply but said: "Everything's ok mate," and climbed off the engine and waited for his driver to join him. As the two of them walked away James surveyed the footplate area. It was well kept, with the boards swept clean. The coal in the tender was piled up and broken into fist-sized lumps. A tin bucket with a brush in it sat in the area beside his wooden seat. The engine front plate controls were cleaned to a shine. Polished with an oily cotton waste pad thought James. The warmth from the firebox made him feel very comfortable. He looked at the water gauge glass. It showed three quarters full. Glancing at the steam pressure gauge it showed 190psi. Perfect he thought. Just perfect.

Eddie sat in his seat opposite James, he was taking a small pinch of snuff and appeared relaxed and at peace with the world. James looking into the firebox at the glowing red fire bed thought it might need a bit more fuel. He stood up and retrieving the long bladed shovel from the tender thrust it into the pile of coal. Taking a good shovel full of coal, he turned and swung the shovel at the firebox aperture. With a loud clang the shovel hit the side of the firebox door, and sent a shower of coal and dust across the footplate boards. James looked at it in dismay.

Eddie smiled at James and laughed saying: "What the hell was that mate?"

Feeling like a right fool and pointing at the firebox, James muttered: "I thought it needed a bit of coal on it."

Eddie laughed again. "Well that won't do it eh," he said.

Getting up from his seat Eddie said: "Here let me show you how it's done."

He took the shovel from James hands and shoved it lightly into the pile of coal. Lifting the shovel he turned and lightly tapped the shovel of coal onto the firebox aperture base. The coal slid of the shovel into the firebox. He repeated this several times and handing the shovel back to his dismayed fireman said: "There. That's how you do it. Little and often, slow and easy."

Just as he finished the demonstration a shunter walked up to the engine. He looked up at Eddie and said: "Your trains formed up ready to go Eddie. Back onto it and I will couple you up."

The guard of their small train of goods wagons strolled over to them and said, "Give us time to get in the van Eddie and we are ready to go."

Eddie nodded ok, and told James to release the tender brake. Unwinding the brake handle anti-clockwise the brake was released. Eddie wound the gear handle into full back gear and lifted the regulator handle. With a short blast from the chimney, the engine moved towards the row of goods wagons. With a sharp clang they hit the wagons buffers. The shunter, using his shunting pole, threw the coupling link onto the engines hook. With a wave he walked back to the shunters' cabin. Eddie wound the gear lever into full forward gear. Looking back towards the brake van James watched the guard climb aboard. He said, "Monkey's in his box mate."

Eddie laughed: "What did you just say?" he asked.

"Monkey's in his box mate," replied James.

Eddie chortled: "Ok. We are ready to go then you cheeky sod!"

They both laughed out loud. Eddie opened the main brake ejector, watching as the brake gauge needles showed 21 inches of vacuum. He lifted the regulator handle gently and the small powerful engine moved forward slowly gaining speed. With the wagons rolling along behind them they moved up the incline towards Reading West Station.

As they went along James sat watching the scenery pass by. He could see into the back gardens of the houses in Salisbury Road, and standing at the back door of one house was a man smoking a cigarette. He watched them as they rolled by. Eddie said with a chuckle: "Look at that poor sod, he is not allowed to smoke indoors, his misses chucked him outside."

They laughed and James said: "Maybe he is a train spotter."

Eddie replied: "No, he has definitely been chucked out poor sod."

They were approaching the starter signal at the end of the incline. With the signal in the stop position Eddie applied the brake. The brake gauge left hand needle fell showing that the vacuum brake was firmly applied. James dropped the firebox door flap. The firebox flap was a half round piece of metal attached to a chain; this could be used instead of the doors. It allowed easier access when firing the engine and also allowed secondary air to enter the firebox. The extra air entering this way helped with combustion.

They sat there waiting, as several fast passenger trains rushed through Reading West Station. Several minutes later with the lines cleared, the signal was dropped giving them permission to move onto the main line. Eddie wound the gear lever into full forward gear and lifting the regulator the engine lunged forward. Dragging the train up the incline they ran over the Oxford Road Bridge and through Reading West Station. James sat enthralled looking down at the Oxford Road as they passed above it. Passing through the station he saw the Tilehurst Road Bridge in front. As they passed under the bridge eventually the Southcote junction came into view. As they approached the signal box they were diverted onto the Coley branch line.

Eddie looked at James and said: "Get ready to catch the staff, mate".

Looking over the side of the engine, he noticed the signalman standing to the side of the signal box holding a large hooped object. He leaned over the side of the cab and caught the hoop with his arm. Turning to the driver, James was told to place it on the tender brake handle. This accomplished they carried on. James stood up and dropping the firebox flap looked into the fire bed. The coal was burning brightly so James turned and picked up the long bladed coal shovel. He thrust it into the pile of coal in the tender and began to fire the engine as Eddie had shown him. He placed two shovelfuls into the backend of the firebox just inside the door. He then shovelled two to the front, two to the side and one to the middle, each time tapping the shovel on the firebox aperture shoe. The shoe consisted of a curved lump of metal that sat in the firebox entrance. Above this was the smoke plate, another curved much larger piece of metal that jutted into the firebox. This helped with secondary air combustion. He looked at the steam gauge, noticing it read 200psi. He then looked at the water gauge glass. It showed 4 inches of water, so opening the water feed handle on the tender, he fed water to the injector mechanism. After this he tapped open the steam handle with his hand brush. This allowed steam to rush into the injector, forcing the water into the boiler. With the injector feed singing nicely he again sat down on his seat and admired the view.

Soon houses and other building came into view and they entered Coley shunting yard. James shut of the water injector and dropped the firebox flap. They slowly ran across the wide yard and passing under the Berkley Avenue Bridge came to a halt outside the shunters' cabin. The guard dismounted from the brake van and walked up to the engine.
Looking up at the driver, he said: "Right, Eddie. We can shunt of these few wagons then have a tea break."
Eddie replied with a short: "OK mate. Let's get it done."
They shunted the few wagons into the various sidings and returned to stop outside the cabin. Eddie applied the brake and James wound on the tender brake. This was necessary to prevent the engine moving if the vacuum brake lost its vacuum. This would happen if the engine stood dormant for an extended period Eddie, taking the tea can with him, climbed off the engine.
He said: "I will make the tea mate, won't be long."
He entered the cabin and James, sitting on the engine looked about the yard confines. Several minutes later Eddie returned with a hot sweet can of tea. James thought; "This is great being served tea by the driver, very strange. What he did not know was that Simmonds Brewery staff issued the rail shunters with a daily bucket of beer. Eddie had had a swift half while waiting for the kettle to boil.

The day seemed to pass fairly fast. After a few more shunting moves they were ready to leave the yard and take a small number of wagons back to the West Reading yard. The run back to the yard was easy to James, who in the short period he had on the footplate, was becoming used to the art of firing the little engine. After shunting the train off into the yard, they took the engine to the loco shed running the fire down low. They left the engine on the coal stage area and after a quick wash in the driver's cabin James retrieved his bike from the bike shed. Cycling home he was immensely pleased with himself. The day had gone well and the driver was good company. He was looking forward to a good week's work with Eddie. Life felt great!

THE COAL YARD

After a successful week working with Eddie Price in the Coley yard James checked the roster before going home Friday evening. He saw that he was rostered on the Reading coal yard in Vastern Road. His driver was Tommy Knibs. The time he was to start on Monday was 6am. He cycled home and wondered what Monday would bring.

After a lazy weekend he retired to his bed early Sunday night. He knew that Monday morning before going to the coal yard he would have to prepare the engine. He had never prepared an engine before and hoped he would not bugger it up. After a restless night's sleep he arose at 4.45am. He brewed a hot pot of tea and then woke his uncle Sid. They sat and drank their tea before leaving the house at 5.30am.

James arrived at work and booked on duty. He looked at the roster board and saw that 9470 was the engine to be prepared. It was on number 3 bay. He walked to the lamp house and collected two lamps. He carried them through the shed to the engine. After placing the lamps on the engine he opened the toolbox on the side of the engine to check that the detonators were in place. He also removed two flare lamps making sure they were filled with paraffin. Climbing up onto the footplate he noticed the mess of coal and ash scattered about the floor area. A coal pick was to one side of the floor area with a tin bucket. In the bucket was a hand brush. A shovel leaned against the coalbunker door. James looked at the steam pressure gauge. It read 100psi. He then checked the water gauge glass. The water level was 2 inches. He then opened the blowdown valve at the base of the gauge glass, watching as the water disappeared. Shutting the valve, the water reappeared back to 2 inches. Satisfied the gauge was reading correct he turned his attention to the flare lamps. He tapped the blower valve open. A hiss of steam propelled smoke out of the smoke box chimney. Opening the firebox door he lit the two flare lamps. Climbing down from the footplate he walked to the front of the engine and climbed up to the smoke box door. Unscrewing the door handle he pulled the door open. Looking inside with the light from the flare lamps, he checked it was clear of cinders and ash. He checked the spark arrester and tube plate. Satisfied all looked OK, he shut the door and winding the handle clockwise locked it. Climbing down he walked back to the footplate area.

Before climbing back onto the footplate he remembered he had to check the sand boxes. Taking the lids from the boxes he noted the sand was low. "Bugger." He did not relish carrying heavy sand buckets from the sand house. But with a sigh he made his way to the sand house and filled two large sand buckets. Struggling with the two sand buckets he staggered back to the engine. He poured the sand into the sand boxes and wearily carried the empty buckets back to the sand house. By now he was feeling very tired. But there was a lot more to do. The driver, Tommy Knibs, arrived as he was climbing back onto the footplate. Tommy was a chap standing about five foot seven. He was of a large stature, and had a face like a bulldog. Not the sort of chap to upset thought James.
Tommy greeted James: "Good morning mate. You started early didn't you?"

James replied: "Yes I thought it wise to get an early start 'cos I've never prepared an engine before."
"Good idea mate, but I am sure you will be OK."
With that said Tommy went off to the shed stores to collect his oil. James surveyed the mess around him; with a strain he lifted the large fire pricker bar from the rear of the cab. He opened the firebox door and pushed the pile of burning coal across the fire grate with the pricker. Satisfied it was spread evenly he began to shovel more coal into the firebox. While doing this he noted that the smoke plate was missing. Shit he remonstrated, now he had to find a smoke plate. Climbing back off the engine he walked into the shed where several dormant engines stood. Climbing up onto one of the engines he spied a smoke plate amongst the coal in the tender. Lifting the heavy metal plate from the coal he carried it back to his engine.

He heaved the plate up onto the footplate following it. He then fitted it into the firebox ring. By now he was sweating heavily. Looking into the firebox he noticed with satisfaction that the fire was burning brightly. Taking hold of the shovel he began to add more coal to the fire bed. With this complete he climbed up onto the engine's coalbunker. With the coal pick he broke the coal into small lumps. He swept the coal from the cab's roof, where it had amassed during the coaling stage. This done he climbed down to the footplate again. Checking the steam gauge he saw it was registering 180 pounds pressure. He looked at the water gauge glass, it showed half a glass full. James opened the water valve at the rear of the cab and watched the water pour out of the injector overflow pipe by the lower step. He then tapped open the steam valve on the front panel. With the injector singing he pulled up the pep pipe from the side of the steps where it hung loose. He swept the odd bits of coal and ash from the floor area and opening the water valve to the pep pipe, washed the floor area with steam and water. Having cleaned the floor area he then hosed down the coalbunker.

With the gauge glass showing three quarters full he shut off the injector. He then climbed down from the engine and jumping into the pit, in a crouching movement he moved under the engine to inspect the ash pan. Looking into the ash pan he could see the red hot fire bed only a few inches above his head. Seeing it was clear of ash he crawled out away from the hot space and climbed from the pit.

As he climbed back onto the engine Tommy was finishing his oiling. "Time to make a can of tea," he said, handing James the tea can.
James went to the drivers' cabin and made the tea. Re-joining the engine it was now time to leave the shed. They made their way to the outgoing line and stopped at the signal post. James climbed off the engine and phoned the signal box. He told them that the 6 o'clock engine for the Vastern Road coal yard was waiting to leave the shed. After waiting several minutes the signal dropped and the driver put the gear lever into the full forward position, Lifting the regulator and with a loud bark from the chimney the engine moved forward. They made their way through Reading Station and were directed to the coal yard entrance line.

There was a falling gradient to the yard and, arriving at the base, James climbed off the engine and set the points to direct them to the shunters' cabin. The engine brake was applied and the driver produced an oilcan. He then poured the oil over the engine control panel. Turning to James with a wad of cotton waste he said: "Clean that lot off fireman, then you can have breakfast."
James stared at the oily mess in dismay. "Fuck it!" he thought. What a mean thing to do. He glared at Tommy but said nothing, but under his breath he muttered to himself: "I am fucked if I am cleaning that lot off with bloody cotton waste."

He waited for Tommy to go into the shunters' cabin Then he put the water injector on, and pulling the pep pipe up from the steps, he hosed the control panel with a jet of steam and water. With a hissing and spluttering noise, the engine cab filled with steam and water. Making sure all the offending oil was washed away, and gasping in the steamy cab, James shut of the pep pipe and injector. He washed his hands in the tin bucket and climbed off the engine.

Walking into the shunters' cabin he glared at Tommy daring him to say a word about how quick he had cleaned the panel. He made a hot sweet cup of tea and gradually his temper cooled. The rest of the shift passed easy as they moved wagons around the yard shunting them into the various sidings. Some sidings were allocated to coal merchants and some to scrap metal merchants. Others were allocated to varied companies.

Terry Forrester had promised James that he would bring a motorbike into the yard for him to look at. James had told Terry that he would buy it from him if he liked it. Terry true to his word turned up at 12 o'clock with a black and silver 350cc Ariel Red Hunter motorcycle.
James admired the shiny black machine.
"Do you want a test ride?" asked Terry.
James looked at the large machine thinking it was a lot bigger than his racing bike.
"Yes. Let's have a go," he replied hesitantly.

James mounted the machine and noticed how heavy it was. Leaning the motorbike to the left he kicked the foot start. The bike roared into life. As he twisted the throttle he pulled in the clutch lever on the handlebar and with his right foot lifted the gear lever into first gear. With the engine ticking over he gradually let out the clutch lever. The bike to James surprise shot forward and racing across the yard he panicked and crashed into a stop block corner. With a resounding bang he hit the stop block and the bike's headlamp shot of and landed on the front mudguard.
""Fuck it," he thought, "I have knackered Terry's bike.
Leaning over the handlebar he tried to retrieve the headlamp. Terry came running toward him laughing but the laugh suddenly stopped as he saw the damage.
"What the fuck have you done to my bike?" he cried.
"Sorry mate, but I couldn't help it. I didn't realise it was so powerful."
Together they managed to replace the headlamp.
Terry asked James: "Do you still want to buy it, mate?"

James replied: "Yes, can you ride it to my house Monday I will have the money ready."

With that agreed he became the owner of the motorcycle. The rest of the shift passed without incident and they were relieved by the afternoon crew at one o'clock. Walking back to the loco shed they booked off duty at 2pm. The rest of the week ran the same as Monday but Tom my did not make anymore mean tasks for James to do, and a good working relationship was established

GENERAL SHUNTING DUTIES

The months to follow were taken up with the same routine of shunting duties in the local goods yards. He was allocated different drivers each month. One month he was working with Arthur (Maggie) Griffith a very good driver with years of experience. Arthur suffered from a stomach ulcer, and some mornings he came to work in great pain. But he never lost his genial good nature and James liked working with him very much.

Another driver was Reggie Kerslake. Reggie was a small Welsh man with a very genial nature. He always called James "Spungle Guts" and always chuckled to himself as he said it.

All the drivers in the shunting links were in their sixties and usually due for retirement. Working with these drivers James was sometimes allowed to take over the driving. He relished these working days and soon became adept in the art of smashing into the goods wagons and sending them shooting across the yard faster than was required. Also sometimes he was rostered to go to Theale Station yard. The job entailed preparing a small 22 class loco and going to the Reading West junction goods yard. Here they backed onto small amounts of goods wagons some with goods for Theale Station yard, and some with waste clinker to tip in the gravel pits in that area.

Firing the engine on these trips was easy. Following the same route as the Coley job but after passing Southcote junction signal box they passed the branch line and carried on along the main line. Arriving at Theale Station they would uncouple the engine and after the signalman set the rail lines, run around the train to the reverse end. This accomplished they then commenced shunting the wagons into their various sidings. The driver sometimes allowed James to do the driving. But the guard told him to take it a bit easier as he was shunting the wagons too hard. One day he hit a wagon so hard, the guard said it went over the top of the stop blocks. But he was sure the guard was winding him up.

After completing the shunting moves they moved the engine to the rear of the station platform. Here they would make their tea and have breakfast. James walked into the station office where sat two young ladies. The older of the two sat at a desk with a typewriter. The other younger girl sat on a desk by the tea kettle.
With a smile on his face James asked: "Morning ladies is the kettle boiling?"

The younger girl smiled and replied: "Yes it should be OK."

James walked by her and squeezed her knee saying: "Thanks my lovely. Can't do without a nice cuppa can we."

She smiled back at him and he noticed she had one tooth missing, but she was still a nice looking girl.

Tea made he returned to the engine. The guard was standing on the engine speaking to the driver.

"You been chatting up the girls fireman?" he enquired.

"No, not really, just been making the tea," James replied.

"Well the young one's ambition is to marry a locomotive fireman," said the guard with a grin.

James laughed saying: "Not this one mate."

Days like this were a common occurrence for several months.

STUCK FOR STEAM

It was an early morning start for James. The job he was on today was the Didcot to Reading goods train. This was a regular job that ran from Monday to Friday moving goods from Moreton goods yard at Didcot to Reading West Junction goods yard and coal to Earley Power Station.

The early morning mist created a damp and dismal facade over the loco shed. The coal smoke from the engines being prepared for the day hung low with no breeze to dispel it. The engine they had today was 9402 a tank locomotive. He wearily searched around the shed confines to find a descent shovel and smoke plate. The problem with preparing the engine was always the loss of tools due to other firemen collecting what they required from the vacant engines. After about 30 minutes of searching he had established a full tool collection. James always started work early to allow for the delay in searching for tools.

His regular driver Joe Lee was on annual leave because his wife had presented Joe with a baby daughter and he was needed at home to help. So his driver for this week was Bill Williams. Bill was a good experienced driver with a demand for professional competence. He was about 40 years age and about 5 foot seven inches tall. He had a friendly nature but did not suffer fools gladly as James was to find out to his discomfort.

With the engine half prepared Bill arrived and greeted James with a curt good morning. They both diligently got the engine ready for the journey to Didcot. James went off to the drivers cabin to make a hot sweet can of tea. He returned to find Bill ready to leave the shed. They drank their tea in silence as they made their way to the west end of the shed. As they waited at the exit signal the guard climbed onto the footplate. He was required to ride on the engine with them to Didcot to act as their guard on the return journey. The footplate on a tank engine the size of a 9402 class is small and James did not have much room to fire the engine. He was aware that he had built a thick layer of coal in the firebox and because they were traveling with just the engine the fire would burn slowly. The signal arm dropped and Bill lifted the regulator to allow the engine to accelerate away to the down relief line and they were soon heading towards Didcot. James sat on the fireman's side of the cab and watched the dark countryside pass by. When the engine ran into the goods yard at Moreton the sun was just lighting the sky, showing dark rain clouds. James opened the firebox doors to inspect the fire. He noticed the fire was burning well and the steam pressure was rising to 200psi. He opened the water valve on the water injector and opened the steam valve. The pressure dropped as the cold water was injected into the boiler.

James washed the coal in the coalbunker to lay the dust, as they would be traveling bunker first towards Reading. The guard and shunters guided Bill back onto the train and coupled up the engine to the wagons. The train was now ready to travel back towards Reading.
James decided it was time to add more coal into the firebox but he was alarmed to find a large lump of coal had wedged itself in the bunker aperture. The signal to leave the yard had fallen and Bill lifted the regulator.
With the train moving onto the up relief line James grabbed the small coal pick from the corner of the cab and tried to break the lump of coal. He was worried that the fire would burn away faster than he could replenish it. With only a small space to work in he could only chip away at the lump and break small pieces off.

Bill was concentrating on the train's momentum and watching for the signals unaware of the problem that was unravelling before him. As the small pieces of coal were chipped away, they began to build a small layer of coal on the footplate so James would clear the coal each time it became a tripping hazard. He opened the firebox door and shovelled the small lumps of coal into the fire. He continued chipping away at the big lump of coal intent on removing the nuisance blockage. Unfortunately he was so concerned in clearing the blockage he did not notice that the steam pressure was dropping back but Bill did.

He leaned over to look at the steam pressure gauge and in a reprimanding tone said: "What are you doing, have you seen the steam pressure? It's only 160psi and the water is in the bottom of the gauge glass!"
James stood up from his crouched position and looked at the steam pressure and water gauge. Bill leaned over towards him and grabbing hold of the firebox door handle pulled it open to reveal a bed of black coal with hardly a flame showing.

"You have blacked the fire in, do you know what you are doing?" Bill remonstrated with a concerned ring to his voice
"Sorry Bill but I had…"
James' apology was cut short by Bill as he again announced: "We will have to stop at Cholsey to recover steam pressure and water, look you have only got 2 inches in the boiler!"
James was well aware of the danger caused by the lack of water as the fusible lead plug in the firebox roof could melt and cause an explosion. The train was slowing gradually as they approached Cholsey Station and Bill brought it to a stop opposite the signal box. The signalman opened his window to enquire what the problem was. Bill leaned out of the cab and shouted loudly in an angry voice. "We need to stop a while to recover steam!" The signalman acknowledged the request and closed the window. James lifted the heavy iron pricker bar from its cradle at the rear of the cab.
He then pushed it into the firebox. With the faint glow of the fire reflecting on his face he raked the fire attempting to improve its ignition. Bill tapped open the blower valve allowing steam to eject from the chimney. This drew air through the firebox improving combustion.

Gradually the fire responded and the steam pressure began to rise. The water however was only showing 2 inches in the gauge glass. James nervously removed the red-hot glowing pricker bar from the firebox and, struggling with care, put it back into its cradle. He was now perspiring and feeling utterly dejected. How could I have been so stupid to fuck the fire up like that, he thought. That bloody great big lump of coal was the fault he conceded.

Bill watched him intently as he struggled to improve the engine's state of affairs. With the steam pressure rising to 200psi James opened the water injector and filled the boiler to the required three quarters full mark in the gauge glass.

Bill sat and stared at him in contempt saying: "Are we ready to continue now? Is your fire burning brighter? Is your steam pressure ok? Are you fit enough?"

Bill was determined to chew out his fireman for the stupid mistake and the effect was being felt intensely by James as he squirmed with embarrassment.

With the steam and water recovered the journey to Reading was accomplished with the large lump of coal eventually demolished into small pieces. But for the next two weeks Bill would not let it rest and made fun of his fireman continually.

Joe returned to work after his two week's leave and James was pleased to get his genial old mate back. After a day's trip to Swindon they were casually walking back to the loco depot after getting relief at Reading West Junction goods yard. James mentioned to Joe what had happened on the Didcot goods train admitting that he had made a bad mistake and that Bill had taken so much umbrage. He confessed he did not know why Bill had made such a fuss about the incident.

Joe nodded his head and replied: "Poor old Bill is going round the bend with worry. His wife is having a baby and Bill is worrying himself silly so you can see why he is so grumpy."
James thought of all these drivers' wives having babies late in life and realized his worries might be the same later on in life.

SWINDON WITH ARTHUR

The cold winter months were behind him now and the warm summer days were a welcome change. Booking off duty one day he noted on the roster board that he was with driver Arthur Hutchins. The job was at 7am the following Monday morning with a goods train to Swindon. Great, he thought, a main line job with a large goods engine at last. Arthur was a driver aged in his late thirties. He was a tall man with dark hair tinged with grey. He rode a big 750CC Royal Enfield Super Meteor motorcycle. A more modern bike than James' 350 Ariel Red

Hunter. Booking on duty Monday James as usual arrived early, at 6.30am. He looked at the roster board and saw that 2856 was the engine allocated to them. The engine was stationed at the rear of the shed on number 9 line. He walked to the lamp house and collected two lamps. Taking them to the engine he placed one to the front and one to the rear. Climbing aboard the engine he saw a mess of coal and clinker spread across the floor area. He turned and opened the lid of the tool chest on the coal tender. He checked that the detonators were in place. He took out a hand brush and coal pick. A decent coal shovel was in place in the tender coal heap. A tin bucket was in position by the pep pipe under his seat. He saw a large smoke plate was also in the coal heap. Glad that all the tools were on the engine he began to prepare it for the days work. First he opened the blow down valve on the gauge glass. The water fell and refilled to 3 inches in the glass. He then climbed along the boiler side towards the smoke box. Here he checked the smoke box was clear of cinders and ash. He also checked the spark arrester. Satisfied everything was OK, he shut the smoke box door and returned along the boiler side to the footplate. He swept and shovelled the debris from the floor area. He noticed the steam pressure gauge showed 120psi. After tapping the blower valve handle open he pulled the firebox door open. He noticed that there was a good bed of fire in the rear of the firebox. Turning around he reached for the pricker bar on the tender.

Heaving it out he pushed it into the firebox and spread the burning coal over the fire bars. After shovelling several heaps of coal onto the fire bed, he closed the flap and began to trim the coal in the tender. When this was completed he crawled into the pit under the engine to check the ash pan. As he emerged from under the engine, his driver Arthur walked up to the engine. His face looked very ashen.
He turned to James and said: "I don't feel to well mate," then he burped loudly.
"You look like shit, Arthur," said James. "What's the matter?"
Arthur burped again and said: "My daft wife nearly poisoned me. She filled a Rum bottle with disinfectant and put it in the bloody pantry. I love the old rum so seeing it on the shelf I took a good swig of it. I didn't know it was bloody disinfectant god I feel fucking rough."
"Are you gonna be ok mate?" asked James with a concerned look on his face.
"Yea. Do our best eh?'" replied Arthur who went off to collect his oil from the stores.
James continued preparing the engine and with 200psi on the steam pressure gauge he washed the footplate clean with the pep pipe. He shovelled more coal into the firebox, building the fire high up to the firebox door, and sloping it to the front. He believed they called it a haycock fire. After checking the sand boxes were filled they were ready to leave the shed. They drove the engine to the rear outgoing signal post by Reading West signal box. After phoning the signal box and announcing that they were the Swindon goods engine the signal dropped and they were given the way to the west Reading goods yard.

They backed onto the goods train and the guard gave Arthur the tally. James rearranged the lamps on the front of the engine, one on the top of the smoke box and one on the left hand buffer. This was the code for a general goods train. Getting back onto the engine he looked into the firebox to check the fire bed. The firebox was much bigger than the small engines he had been working on. He began to build up a good bed of fire at the rear of the firebox. This allowed him to fire the engine, as driver Eddie Price had showed him.

By hitting the shovel on the mound of coal just inside the firebox ring, he was able to direct the coal where it was needed. He checked the water gauge glass. It showed three quarters full. The steam gauge needle was showing 200psi. Great thought James, now we are ready for the fray. The guard gave them the tip to proceed. Arthur, still looking like death warmed up, wound the gear handle into full forward gear. He opened the big brake ejector, the brake gauge needles showing 21 inches of vacuum. They were ready to go. Arthur lifted the regulator handle and with a sharp bark from the chimney the train moved forward.

Gathering speed they moved along the goods line towards Scours Lane starter signal. As they approached the signal post, the signal dropped giving them access to the down relief main line. Arthur opened the regulator further and wound back the gear handle, changing the valve gear stroke. This made the engine gather speed and soon they were rattling through Tilehurst Station at a faster rate. James satisfied the engine was maintaining a good head of steam looked out at the scenery. He watched as the river Thames on their right hand side came into view. The sun made the water shine and the trees along the banks look green and fresh. He was filled with elation, what a great job this is, he surmised, and getting paid for it as well.

Firing the engine steady and often he maintained a good head of steam. The 28 class goods engine pulled the goods train effortlessly and soon they were racing through Pangbourne Station. Cholsey and Goring stations were passed at a steady pace and then they were into Didcot Station. Here the train was directed onto the main line towards Steventon. The rail lines to Swindon from Didcot were two main lines used by express trains and slow goods trains. Therefore if a fast train was due the goods trains were diverted onto relief spur lines. One relief line was at Steventon Station. The other was at Wantage and Challow. This made the journey to Swindon a slow process for goods trains, sometimes standing in the relief lines for 30 minutes waiting for the main line to clear.

As the train passed Didcot James noted that they were being diverted on to the relief spur at Steventon. Arthur applied the vacuum brake steadily as they ran into the relief spur. James dropped the firebox flap and put on the main injector water feed. The boiler pressure was 240psi and a wisp of steam began to issue from the relief blow off valve on top of the boiler. This was a waste of steam and energy but the steam blow of safety valve suddenly gushed steam into the atmosphere with a loud hiss. James kept the water injector feed running and soon the steam blow off safety valve closed. The water gauge glass showed over three quarter full so he closed the injector feed and closed the firebox ash pan dampers. They stood at the signal for about 20 minutes, after watching several fast passenger trains flash by, the signal dropped allowing them access to the main line. James opened the ash pan dampers and dropped the firebox flap. He began firing the engine, shovelling coal into the firebox creating columns of smoke. The steam pressure gauge kept steady at 230psi. As the engine pulled the wagons out of the spur it encountered a slight uphill gradient. This made the beat of the engine to bark loudly out of the chimney. The sound from the engines chimney reminded James of the Frank Sinatra song *Love and marriage, go together like a horse and carriage, this I tell you brother, you cant have one without the other* having four beats to the bar. As the train gathered speed the beats ran into a fast cacophony of sound. James closed the firebox flap and leaned over the side of the engine to admire the passing scenery. As they passed Wantage Road Station he noticed a small steam engine on the platform being displayed for the public.

"Hey Arthur, what's a steam engine doing on the platform?" he asked his driver.

Arthur replied: "That little engine used to run a train from Wantage Road Station into the village, which is some distance away. But the line's been closed so all that's left is the engine. Makes a nice reminder of times gone by though."

Well, thought James, you learn something every day.

They had a good run rattling along towards Challow. They passed the little station and soon James noticed a big white horse carved into the hills.

He turned to Arthur again: "What's the horse carving about mate?"

Arthur turned his gaze away from the front of the engine and looking at his fireman said: "It's the white horse of Uffington, carved by ancient Celts. There is also an ancient fort up there too."

He then returned his attention to the line and signals in front. This is like a mystery train tour thought James. The next station was Shriveham, which they passed at a good speed. The engine James thought was responding well to his firing method. He had a good head of steam. The water gauge was kept at three quarters full by occasional use of the water injector. With the engine having a full head of steam they were diverted into Swindon goods yard. James dropped the flap and closed one damper to help reduce the fire.

As they came to a stop in the yard Arthur put on his jacket and thrust a sheath of papers into James hand. "I'm off mate. You will be all right won't you? Give these papers to my relief, OK."

With that said he climbed off the engine and disappeared in the direction of Swindon Station. James sat on the engine feeling nervous. I bloody hope the new crew comes soon he pondered. To his relief after about fifteen minutes the driver and fireman arrived. He greeted the driver and fireman. "Am I glad to see you mate. My driver's gone sick so I'm here on my own."

He handed the driver the papers and with a curt goodbye climbed of the engine. He then headed the same route as Arthur, towards Swindon Station. He arrived at the station by walking along the lines. He made his way to platform two. This was the up main line platform for Reading trains. As he stood there several passengers congregated on the platform. On man edged up to him and softly said: "Excuse me. Are there any trains due this minute?"

James looked up the line and said: "No mate looks all clear."

With the words hardly out of his mouth the man jumped off the platform onto the track. James heart raced, what the fuck is he doing, he thought in alarm. The man bent over in the middle of the rails and picked up something and jumped back on the platform. Grinning the man waved a five pound note in his face. "My lucky day, eh mate?"

With this said he walked away to the other end of the platform! "You lucky bastard", James riled, "I should have seen that".
The Reading train soon arrived and James gratefully jumped aboard and found a vacant carriage. He sank down into the soft seat and as the train pulled out of the station dozed off. Arriving in Reading Station he walked to the loco depot and mounting his motorbike raced home in the knowledge he had done the Swindon trip easily

LAMBOURNE BRANCH BOMB TRAIN

It was on a bright sunny spring day that James was rostered to work with Driver Gordon Evans. The workday involved traveling to Newbury with a 2200 class steam locomotive. On arrival at Newbury they were to travel over the Lambourne branch line to Welford Park RAF depot, to collect an MOD train. On arrival at Newbury goods yard Driver Evans told James he had to make a quick visit to the town centre. Leaving James in charge of the engine he made a quick exit in the direction of the town centre. After a half hour he returned looking very pleased with himself. They waited in the yard while a train was assembled to take to Welford Park. The guard coupled them onto the few wagons and eventually the signalman set the points to let them travel through Newbury Station and onto the Lambourne branch line. The little 2200 locomotive was ideal for the Lambourne branch line and after traveling through Stockcross and Bagnor Station, they ran down an incline to Boxford Station. The next station was Welford Park and upon arriving there the little train was diverted into the RAF depot. The train was uncoupled and they were directed onto a longer train of open wagons.

The guard came up to the train and announced to Driver Gordon Evans that the wagons contained armaments, meaning BOMBS!
Driver Evans looked at the train and said to James: "We have got a heavy train here fireman, so make sure we have a good head of steam."
James looked into the firebox and began to build up a thick bed of burning coal. The chimney gushed a column of black smoke and as the steam pressure went up to 200psi a feather of steam began to issue from the safety valve. James dropped the firebox flap to prevent the safety valve erupting further.

They waited a few minutes then the signal dropped giving them access to the branch line. The driver wound the gear lever into full backward motion. The engine was now traveling tender first toward Newbury. The engine started back with loud barks of noise from the smoke stack. The train pulled out of the depot slowly and then gradually gathered speed as they passed the Welford Park Station. The little engine kept a good head of steam as the coal in the firebox burned with a bright orange glow. The water level in the gauge glass stayed at three quarters full. James was satisfied the little engine was performing well. As he looked over the coal tender, he could se the rail line was beginning to become a rising gradient. As they ascended the gradient the train became slower. The little engine was becoming slower and slower until half way up the gradient they came to a full stop. With the regulator open fully, the engine refused to move.

Driver Evans was looking a worried man. "I told you we are grossly overloaded," he repeated to James. "Look. We are buggered now, the engine won't move at all!"

The guard had climbed out of his brake van and came running up to the engine.

"What's the matter Driver has the engine broken down?" he asked.

"No. Of course not, we are overloaded for this small engine," replied Gordon. "This engine is not powerful enough to pull such a heavy train."

The guard looked perplexed and asked: "What do you think we should do about it then?"

Gordon, with a sigh of resignation, said: "There is only one answer to that question, we will have to run back half a mile or so, and take a fast run at this gradient."

The guard with a worried voice said: "Do you think that's wise driver?"

Gordon glared at the guard and said: "Well if you have a better idea, I am all bloody ears!"

The guard, noticing the hard edge to Gordon's reply, agreed to the plan of action. He hurried back to the safety of his brake van and waited for Gordon to reverse the train.

Gordon looked over at James who was now sitting nonchalantly on his wooden seat. "Are you ready for this then?" he asked.

James shrugged his shoulders and responded with a laugh. "Well there is a first time for everything ain't there? So let's do it."

He had never known this to happen before and thought it hilarious. The film *The Titfield Thunderbolt* came to his mind. All we need now would be Sid James to turn up with his bloody big steamroller, he chuckled silently to himself. He could have pulled us up the bloody gradient.

Gordon wound the gear handle into forward motion as the engine was in reverse mode. He gently opened the regulator and the train began to run back down the gradient. They allowed the train to run onto a level stretch of line. Gordon then applied the brake bringing the train to a stop. James dropped the firebox flap and began to shovel more coal onto the hot orange-flamed fire bed. He lifted the flap into the closed position. He then put on the water injector allowing the water to rise in the gauge glass. When he was satisfied with the results he nodded to Gordon saying: "We have a good head of steam and the fire has been burning fine, so when you are ready lets go for it."

Gordon wound the gear lever back into reverse and lifted the regulator into the full open position. The little engine exploded with energy and with the wheels slipping slightly they headed back to the bloody gradient. The chimney blasted dark smoke and bright sparks as the little engine gathered speed. As they approached the rising rail line the engine did not falter. It gathered speed with Gordon looking over the tender and grimacing at the wind blowing coal dust into his face. James sat on his seat watching the sleepers slide by underneath the engine. He tried to keep his face shielded from the coal dust being blown off the tender. As the train got nearer the summit of the gradient it began to falter, slowing slightly. When they passed Stockcross and Bagnor the little engine slowed a bit but kept going. The line now turned into a falling gradient and as the rear of the train came over the summit it began to push the engine forward at an alarming speed. The train was now being pushed by the weight of the BOMBS as it headed toward Newbury Station. Driver Gordon was beginning to apply the brakes, but they had no affect. The wheels slid along the rails generating sparks as he desperately tried to gain control. He looked at James with alarm etched on his face. "Fuck this" thought James because he knew the line dropped sharply after the next signal. The distant signal had been on which meant the next one would be at danger. He also knew if they could not stop, the train would hurtle into the station stop blocks in the rear platform. The results did not bear thinking about, as Newbury Station and themselves would cease to exist.

Driver Gordon shouted at James saying: "Can you climb over the side onto the steps and get sand out of the sand boxes, then throw it onto the rails?"
James did not need telling twice. In desperation he climbed over the side of the engine and standing on the iron steps removed the sand box covers. Hanging onto the rail at the side of the steps with one hand, he threw handfuls of sand onto the rails under the engines wheels. Gradually the wheels stopped sliding and the train slowly came to a halt in front of the danger signal. Climbing back onto the footplate he grinned at Gordon and said: "Well that fucking worked!"
He added: "If that had not worked I was ready to jump off mate."
But Gordon was not smiling, he said: "I think I would have followed you. We are seriously overloaded with this bloody train."
They both sat there with the tension subsiding. After waiting several minutes the signal dropped and they were directed into the Newbury Station goods yard. The train was uncoupled and they took the engine back to Reading loco depot. James could not get home fast enough. He did not ever want to repeat that day.

ALLAN MCCROHAN

The spring weather turned into warm summer sunshine and after working with Arthur for several months. His wife did not try to accidently poison him again and they enjoyed a good working relationship. James was allocated another driver. In May 1958 he was rostered to work with driver Alan McCrohan, Alan was a man of about 38 years of age. He stood about 5ft 8 inches and was a very fit looking man with a sturdy frame. Alan loved to work long hours and make good his wage packet. James liked to work with Alan because his shoebox began to fill nicely again.

Booking on duty at 12pm on a Thursday they were rostered to work the same old goods trip to Swindon. The engine allocated to them was 2830. James was becoming quite adept at firing the 2800 class engines, which were the common mode of engine for these jobs. The day was warm with some cloud cover, which made firing the engine very pleasant. Not to hot and not to cold, just perfect to work in the open cab of the big engine.

After climbing on the footplate of the engine James was pleased to find it had already been prepared for them. Alan soon arrived and climbing onto the footplate he winked at James and said: "Are you OK for a long day mate?" Alan suffered from a slight lisp when he spoke James noted.

"If there is a chance Alan, I am all for it," replied James.

"Good, let's start the day with a nice cup of tea then, shall we?"

He handed James his tea can after pouring a small tin of tea and sugar into it. When he came back with the tea made it was time to leave the shed and travel to the goods yard by the East Reading gas works. They vacated the shed, from the east end signal post and travelled tender first through Reading Station. After passing through the station they were directed to the southern railway where the empty coal wagons were waiting in the gas works yard. After backing onto the wagons, the guard appeared and after coupling them up gave Alan the tally.

"We have got 50 empty wagons mate, nice light easy train today," Alan said to James.

With the guard safe in his brake van it was a few minutes before the starter signal dropped giving them access to the main line. Alan released the brakes and with the regulator opened wide the engine moved forward. The line out of the southern yard was on an incline and the big engines chimney belched a column of black smoke and sparks as it pulled the wagons up the incline and through the station. The signalman then diverted them onto the relief down main line.

James looked at the steam pressure gauge, the needle showed a good 220psi. He looked at the water gauge glass, it showed half full, so he opened the water injector and the water began to rise to three quarters full. After using the pep pipe to wet down the coal tender he shut the injector off. The train was now rattling along at a good fast rate and Tilehurst Station was soon passed by. James leaned over the side of the engine admiring the view. He always enjoyed the goods train trips because it gave him time to gaze at the countryside, which he found fascinating. Its verdant green colours mingled with the river Thames waters sparking in the summer sun. What job could be better, he thought. Many of the older drivers used to say that the reason their wages were so low was because they enjoyed the job so much They said they would have done the job for free but it didn't put food on the table.

The train was pulling nice and fast and soon they had passed Didcot Station. They were directed onto the Swindon main line but as always with the slow goods they were directed into the goods loop at Steventon. Travelling slowly up the loop line they eventually came to a stop at the end of the line, and waited at the signal post for the main line to clear of fast traffic.

Driver Alan looked at his watch and with a smile said: "If we are delayed here and further on at Challow, we should be OK for some overtime, that's if there is another train we can work back from Swindon."

James nodded in agreement and with the firebox flap dropped and the water injector on. He was sat leaning over the side of the engine with his sleeves rolled up, trying to catch the sun on his white arms, hoping for a tan. The warm sun was very pleasant and as he sat there he began to doze. He was rudely brought back to consciousness as the signal dropped with a clatter. Alan wound the gear lever into full forward gear and lifted the regulator. The engine responded with a loud bark from the chimney as they swung out onto the main line. The engine picked up speed as Alan expertly adjusted the gear lever and soon they were again rattling along at a good speed.

But as expected they were again sent into the goods loop at Challow. As they pulled up to the signal post at the end of the loop line James looked at his watch. The time showed 7pm. They had been on duty for 7 hours. The signalman kept them in the loop for twenty minutes and at 7.20pm he dropped the signal giving them access to the main line. The train ran passed Shrivenham and soon the Swindon goods yard came into sight. James fired the engine sparingly as they pulled into the goods loop. He had maintained a good haycock fire and the engine had steamed perfectly. Arriving at the goods yard their relief crew climbed aboard. James spoke to his relief fireman saying: "You have got a good engine here mate, it steams nice and easy." That information imparted he climbed off the engine followed by his driver.

The pair of them went into the loco men's small cabin and made a hot sweet can of tea. They sat there for about 30 minutes, and then picking up the phone Alan phoned the control office.
"Hello, this is the Reading crew of the 3pm Reading train, have you got any traffic going to the Reading area that needs a relief crew?"
The control staff were speaking to him and James heard him say: "Yes OK that will do us, 45 minutes did you say? Right that's fine. Thank you."
Alan put down the phone and gave James a thumbs up gesture. "We have got to wait for a goods train coming up from the Severn tunnel area, should be a 30 minute delay. But its not for the Reading area, it's for Banbury," James grinned.
"Bloody good money spinner. We might make two or three hour's overtime," replied James.
Alan smiled and said: "Might as well make another brew. We have a long wait and I am getting dry sitting around here."
They brewed up another can of tea and sat waiting for the Severn tunnel train to arrive. The time waiting went by slowly and eventually a goods train pulled up on the down goods line opposite their yard. Alan went over to the engine and said: "Are you the train for Banbury driver?"
The driver replied with a broad welsh accent: "Yes mate. Are you our relief?"

Alan replied: "Yes. That's us." He climbed aboard followed by James. The engine impressed James, as it was a Hall class engine, 6959 Peatling Hall. The Hall class engines he reasoned were excellent locomotives. Very versatile, they were used on passenger trains frequently, as well as goods trains. He surveyed the footplate. He noticed that the firebox contained the haycock type fire burning well up to the firebox door. The fireman also said in abroad welsh voice: "Lovely little steamer mate, no trouble at all." He then climbed of the engine and followed his driver to the cabin.

James looked at the coal in the tender and to his satisfaction saw that it contained good welsh hard coal. The coal had been broken into fist size lumps, a sign of a good fireman thought James. The footplate was nice and tidy. It had been swept clear of any loose coal fragments and washed clean with the pep pipe. The wooden boards were nearly white. The time was now 10.15pm. The overtime "ka-ching" of money had started to sound in his ears. Every hour now was time and a half. Alan was looking pleased as well. After waiting for the guard to change, the signal dropped and they went out onto the main line. Firing the engine steadily and keeping the haycock shaped fire, the engine responded by steaming well. Clattering along at a good rate of speed they passed Shrivenham Station and soon were passing Chai low and Wantage road. The light had diminished now and they were immersed in inky darkness.

The signals shone green in front of them as they rattled pass Steventon and Milton. At Didcot they were switched east onto the Oxford main line. Heading toward Appleford Station the line curved to the left and as they approached the darkened station James to his alarm saw a red light directly in front of them. "Fuck!" he thought. It must be a stationary train. He shouted loudly to Alan "RED LIGHT MATE! RIGHT IN FRONT!"

Alan instantly applied the brake but they were traveling to fast to stop. As they approached the red light traveling at an alarming speed it turned to green. James shouted to Alan: "Green light now mate!" As the lit up station platform came into sight James saw a member of staff standing on the platform with a lamp in his hand. The lamp now showed a clear light.

James leaned out of the engines side and shouted "Arsehole you made me shit!!" He turned to Alan and shakily said: "What's that all about?"

Alan replied: "It's probably a check signal to warn us of a line hazard."

He was right. As they moved a further half-mile they saw a bunch of trackside workers standing back to let them pass. "It looks like a bank earth slip," said Alan. "No harm done."

He added with a grin. "Bloody hell I thought we were running into the rear of a train. I nearly shit a brick," Alan laughed.

Soon they were passing Hinksey goods yard and Oxford Station came into view. Running through the station Alan advised James that the line here contained many upward gradients, so he began to fire the engine a bit heavier, making sure the fire shape remained haycock style. As they passed Kidlington the engine began to labour, creating columns of smoke. The line here was on a steep incline. They passed Aynho, and Banbury Station appeared in sight. James tidied the footplate. He trimmed the coal in the tender and brushed the footplate clear of coal spillage. Nice and tidy for our relief crew he thought. As the train ran into the platform they came to a halt at the far end under the starter signal.

A lone person stood on the platform watching them as they came to a stop. James put on his coat and slung his lunch bag over his shoulder getting ready to vacate the footplate. The lone person walked across the platform and climbed aboard the engine. He spoke to Alan saying: "Sorry boys, I haven't got a fireman with me, seems he didn't turn in for his shift, so are you OK to go through to Woodford Halse, with me as a pilotman?"
Alan replied: "Yes I am OK with that."
He turned to James and said: "Are you alright to go on to Woodford mate?"
James looked wearily at him and asked: "Where the bloody hell is Woodford Halse?"

The other driver said, "It's on the LMS line and is about 30 miles from here."
With a look of exasperation due to his weariness, he said: "Yeah. I am alright with that."
The new driver sat in Alan's seat and took control of the engine and Alan stood behind him. The signal at the end of the platform dropped with the light turning green. James reluctantly took off his lunch bag and coat and began to fire the engine again. His arms were aching with exhaustion and his enthusiasm for overtime pay was rapidly becoming less.

The driver piloted them too Woodford Halse taking care not to force the train along to fast. This helped to make the firing of the engine less tiresome. As they arrived at the goods yard the wagons were uncoupled and the staff in the yard informed them that they were required to return the engine to Banbury loco depot. James looked at his watch. The time was 12.15am. They had now been on duty for 12 hours. The trip back to Banbury didn't take long and the engine was put into Banbury loco depot at about 12.45.

The two of them walked to Banbury Station and enquired if there was a train due, that was stopping at Reading Station that time in the morning. The reply from the station staff was: "Yes mate. It happens to be a fish train, and it should be due now."
The train pulled into the station 15 minutes later and smelled exactly like fish.
"Blimey mate don't that really stink," remarked Alan.
"The stink of fish isn't going to stop me getting on," said James and getting into one of the carriages he dived into a warm comfy seat and began to doze. As he dozed he vaguely saw Alan collect up a bundle of old newspapers that had been left in the carriage. He fashioned these into the shape of a ball and tied them securely with pieces of string that he had also found. He tapped James on the shoulder saying: "Come on mate. Let's play a game of football."
James stared at him in amazement. "Bloody football!" he cried. You must be joking. I have barely got the strength to stand upright, let alone play bloody football Alan. Where do you get your energy from?"
Alan laughed and kicking the make shift ball out into the corridor said: "You youngsters have not got any endurance."
James knew that Alan used to play football for Reading football club at Elm Park and was still an enthusiastic player. James thought: "Fucking football! Let me sleep!"
The fish train arrived in Reading Station and by the time they had walked to the loco shed they booked of duty at 2am. A 14-hour shift had been worked. James was very glad he could ride home on his motorbike and was soon in his warm comfortable bed by 2.30am.

The sun was just starting to break through a low cloud cover when he awoke. The weak rays of the sun shone through his bedroom curtains. He forced his eyes open to look at the big alarm clock. The time showed 8.30am Lovely, he thought to himself. He reasoned he had slept a deep sleep for 6 hours and now felt refreshed. Climbing out of the warm confines of the bedcovers he dressed and went into the kitchen to make a hot cup of sweet tea. He carried the tea into the living room and sat in the big comfy chair to drink it. After he had sipped his tea for a while, his mother came down the stairs and looking at him she said: "You are up early. Are you going somewhere?"

"Yes, I think I may go into town and get a Buddy Holly record, *That will be the day*, his latest one," he replied.

His mother looked at him quizzically saying: "You'll be lucky, the shops are closed today."

James looked at her in surprise and replied: "What do you mean? Shops don't close on a Saturday Ma." He laughed at her silly remark.

"It's not Saturday, you doughnut. It's Sunday today," his mother said with a smile on her face. "You must have been exhausted, because you slept all through Saturday. I had to look at you several times to make sure you were ok. Sleeping like a baby you were."

He looked at her with a questioning gaze. "You got to be kidding me Ma? I didn't sleep that long."

His mother nodded her head saying: "Yes you did."

He was completely stunned. How the hell did I manage that fiasco? Slept for hours and hours. The rest of the day he was in a quandary, unable to believe it possible.

SHED DUTIES 1958

All firemen were sometimes allocated to work on shed duties. The work consisted of driving the incoming engines onto the coal stage area. Here the fire residue would be cleared from the firebox and ash pans. Then the engine's coal tender would be filled. The engines would then be driven to their places of need. Some to have their boilers washed out and others to be prepared for the next days work.

James was rostered on the shed duties with driver Jack Webber. He looked at the roster board and noticed it was a night shift. He was required to start on the next Monday. "That's good because I will have a free day until 9pm," he thought.

With this in mind he arranged with his old cleaner mate Bob to go to see the film *Bridge on the River Kwai*. The film was at the Odeon cinema afternoon matinee. Bob was on a night shift as well so they arranged to go already dressed for work. On Monday afternoon he dressed in his grubby overalls, heavy army boots, serge jacket and oil cap. With his lunch haversack across his shoulder he caught a bus into town where he met Bob. The girl in the Odeon pay kiosk gave them a quizzical look but issued the tickets without a comment. They sat in the front rows and enjoyed the film very much. After the film finished they walked to the loco depot in Great Knollys Street and booked on duty.

They were both early for their shifts but thought the film was worth it. The dark evening air was chilly and rain was beginning to fall, making the night's working conditions a cold wet affair. James sat in the driver's cabin chatting to the other firemen until 10pm, and then he made his way to the coal stage premises. Alfie Bottin and his big ginger-haired mate were on the coal stage tipping area. Alfie was a very genial chap, slight of build but very fit. He used to stop and talk to the young cleaners when he came on duty, always praising his son, who he was very proud of. His mate was a big ginger-haired chap who towered over him. They both loved playing cards and encouraged the drivers to join them. This meant the firemen had the opportunity of driving the engines about the shed, before and after being serviced.

When James reached the coal stage area he walked into the driver and fireman's cabin. The room was quite large with a big wooden table in the centre; wooden benches were on each side. These were painted dark brown, which did not add any sparkle to the dark discoloured interior. The walls were painted yellow that had accumulated years of grime, mainly due to the huge coal fire that burned ferociously in the corner of the room. The fire filled the grate rising at least two foot up the chimney. Of course, in this area there was no shortage of fuel. The door remained permanently open; the fire created so much heat the door being closed became unnecessary.

As the drivers and firemen entered the cabin James recognised a few of them Jack Webber his driver was a tall upright person with the bearing of a military man. He wore spectacles and spoke in a clipped manner, but he was a very genial natured man. Driver Hector Doe was an older looking dark featured man. Fair-haired fireman Ron Fry with a ready smile, and Bill (chinky) Goodal a very experienced fireman, slim of build with dark features. As they came in the tea was made before work commenced.

James was eager to fetch the steam engines from the incoming line. In the rain he trudged over to the line that was at the left hand side of the shed. He climbed onto the first engine. It was 6960 Raveningham Hall. He peered at the steam pressure gauge. It read 180psi. The water gauge glass showed half full. He opened the firebox door and the fire bed glowed a dull red. With the fire's red glow illuminating his frame he pulled the big ejector handle downwards, raising the vacuum brake gauge needles to show 21 inches of vacuum. He closed the ejector and applied the brake. He unwound the coal tender brake, and stepped back to the driving side of the engine. James kicked the cylinder drain cock lever by his foot, closing the valve. Turning the gear handle clockwise he put the gears in full forward motion. He lifted the regulator handle and with a loud blast from the chimney exhaust, the big engine moved forward. Slightly worried at the engines quick response James closed the regulator. The engine moved abruptly towards Cow Lane Bridge. As the engine passed over the points to the coal stage he applied the brake. The engine halted and he climbed down onto the trackside. With the cold rain dripping off his peaked cap he ran towards the point lever. He grabbed hold of the big handle and pulled it towards himself, listening to the snap of the points as they changed direction into the coat stage. He ran back to the engine hoping the brakes would hold, as the track was on a decline. The rails fell towards the coal stage. Sometimes making the engines difficult to stop, when they were low in steam pressure. He climbed back onto the footplate and saw with a sigh of relief that the brake pressure was still holding, despite the low steam pressure. He reversed the gear handle and released the brake. With a slight lift of the regulator the engine moved slowly towards the coal stage. As the engine moved towards the engines already being serviced he applied the brake bringing the large buffers together gently.

Brimming with confidence he went back to bring the other engines onto the coal stage. The engines were soon serviced and taken away to their places of need in the shed. Some went to the boiler washout bays and the others to areas to be prepared for work in the morning. Without much to do after 1.30am the drivers sat and read books or newspapers. The older firemen went into the coal stage workers' cabin to play cards with Alfie and his big mate.

James sat and dozed by the big fire. About 4.30am Jack laid down his newspaper and turned to James. He shook his shoulder saying: "Wake up mate I've a little job for you."
James stirred trying to open his sleepy eyes. "What sort of job Jack?" he mumbled.
"There is a tank engine by the coal stage line that needs preparing for the morning shift, so run it up to the coal stage, and raise steam in it."
James put his coat on and pulled his cap down over his eyes. The rain outside was pouring down fairly heavy and he did not relish leaving the warm cabin. As he made his way towards the bottom of the coal stage track he saw a tank engine 9406 standing there. With the rain dripping off his cap he climbed into its warm cab glad of the shelter. He looked at the water in the gauge glass. It only showed an inch of water. Looking at the steam pressure he saw it was very low, 120psi. The engine was facing west. This meant that if he was to drive it up the coal stage bank the water would run to the front of the boiler, therefore exposing the fusible lead plug in the firebox. Bugger that he thought it's too dangerous to do what Jack had asked. He climbed off the engine and made his way back to the warm cabin. Jack was getting ready to move a Hall Class engine to one of the sidings in the shed, and as he watched James approach him, he said: "Have you moved it already?"
James nervously replied: "No Jack. I think the water is to low to take it up the bank, its not safe."
Jack glared at him and responded in an irritated manner: "What do you mean not safe? Look if you can't do it, you take this engine away for me and I will do it!"
So with that agreed James climbed on the engine and moved it into the shed. He returned to the coal stage to see that Jack had moved the engine up the bank. He was busily shovelling coal into the firebox trying to raise the steam pressure. The blower was blowing clouds of black smoke out of the chimney. The sound of metal against metal resounded as he built the fire bed.

Suddenly there was a loud sounding detonation and the engine and Jack disappeared in a cloud of steam and smoke. James stared at the scene in shock, hoping with horror that Jack would be OK. From out of the cloud of steam and smoke Jack emerged with his glasses obscured with water and soot. He took off his glasses and wiped them clean. He did not say a word but James thought he heard him mumble, "Fuck it!'

Jack stumbled down the bank towards him and said: "Well that engine is fucked, I am off to tell Wally," and he briskly walked towards the shed, with the tidings of bad news to be announced in the foreman's office. Obviously the lead plug in the firebox roof had melted. James took no satisfaction in knowing that he had been correct. But Jack had not listened.

When James was rostered to work on shed duties again, it was a cold morning in January 1959. He arrived at work at 5.45am. The morning was dark with a sharp frost in the air. He was glad to enter the coal stage cabin to escape the cold. He sat by the big fire and warmed his frozen hands. His driver for today was John Rowel a man aged about 40. One of their jobs for the day was to remove the empty coal wagons from the coal stage, and replace them with full ones. The wagons did not require moving until 11am as Alfie had two full wagons on the coal stage to empty. So James helped in driving the serviced engines to the shed bays. At 10am John decided to begin shunting the full wagons into a group of five. Making them ready to push up into position on the coal stage. James put on his serge jacket, tied a scarf round his neck and pulled his cap low on his forehead. He followed John over to the 9400 class tank engine that stood at the bottom of the coal stage bank. He climbed onto the engine and began to build the fire. The warmth of the cab was welcome on this bitterly cold day. He raised the steam pressure to 180psi. After making sure the water in the gauge glass was three quarters full he climbed down onto the trackside and looked for a shunting pole. The icy cold wooden pole made his fingers tingle as he picked it up. Walking along the row of full coal wagons he counted five and using the hook on the shunting pole uncoupled the sixth.

James sauntered back to the engine and said to John: "Wagons are ready mate."
He climbed up into the cab for a brief warming of his frozen hands.
"Right. We can go up onto the coal stage and collect the empties then," John replied.
He put the gear lever in reverse and moved the engine to the base of the coal stage slope. James reluctantly climbed off the warm engine and pulled the lever to set the track to the empty wagons. He walked up the slope as the engine moved by him to come to a halt against the first wagon. James trudged along the side of the wagons, unpinning the brakes and lifting the heavy couplings onto their hooks. He noticed there were two wagons still on the coal stage tipping point.
He called to Alfie: "We are ready to remove the wagons, Alfie."
The reply was: "Hang on a minute, we haven't emptied this one, I will let you know when we are ready."
James climbed onto the coal stage floor. The floor was covered in steel plates that made the coal bins move with ease. He watched as Alfie and his mate shovelled the coal into the bins. Alfie turned to face him and said with a smile: "You look bloody froze mate, when we are ready we will take the brakes off these two wagons and couple them up for you."
James thanked him and walked back to the engine. John leaned over the side of the cab watching him approach. He also told him: "You look bloody cold. Get up here and warm yourself."
He didn't need telling twice and clambered up into the warm cab to warm his frozen hands. He sat relishing the warmth until Alfie shouted: "Right mate, we have finished so you can take them away, the brakes are off and the couplings are joined."
James grudgingly climbed off the warm engine and walked down the bank to the catch point lever. He pulled the lever towards himself and sat on his heels. He

found that this was the easiest way to hold the lever tight and keep the point gap closed. The problem was that he was looking back, away from the engine. Holding the cold steel lever with one hand, he waved to John behind him to let him know he was OK to bring the empty wagons down. Sitting on his haunches he felt comfortable keeping the point gap closed. He heard the hiss of the engine steam cylinders and the rumbling noise as the engine passed by him. The gap between him and the engine was too small he thought, as the engine's wheels rolled noisily passed him. Then to his dismay no wagons were to be seen. The engine had passed him and was steaming towards the long incoming rail track. John was peering intently forward to make sure the track was clear of incoming engines. James glanced over his left shoulder to see to his horror that the five empty wagons were running down the slope, accelerating rapidly. He realised with bewilderment that he had forgotten to couple the wagons to the engine. In panic he shouted loudly to John to warn him of an impending crash if the wagons were to hit the engine. But John was so intent on looking forward that he did not hear him. He was completely unaware of the wagons now hurtling down the slope.

James let go of the lever and stood up. He cupped his hands to his mouth and hollered as loud as he could, trying to get John's attention. The first large metal wagon flew by him and James in a fit of terror ran. Listening to a deafening thunder of metal behind him. He ran down the bank and jumped over the rails and inspection pit with a leap that would have made an athlete proud. The rending crashing noise stopped. He turned around and the site of five wagons set at all weird angles met his gaze. Some wagons had fallen towards the engines standing in the coal stage line. Two more were at an angle towards the pit he had just jumped across, and one was stuck on the catch point's sleepers. James dejectedly walked towards the engine where John sat, dumfounded at the sight before him.
James looked up at John and shakily mumbled: "Well we have fucked that up mate, haven't we!"
With a withering stare John replied: "What do you mean 'we'? You fucked that up."
Then with a more sympathetic tone said: "You better go and tell the foreman what you have done. He won't be very pleased."
James traipsed to the foreman's office in dread of a bollocking. He tapped on the doors small flap. The flap opened and Charlie Alder the shed foreman peered out. "What can I do for you young man?" he asked with a convivial tone in his voice. James replied hesitantly: "I am sorry Charlie, I've got five wagons off the line on the coal stage."
Charlie was a quiet mannered man and he did not appear worried. He looked fixedly at the young fireman and said: "You better go and tell the fitters they are needed at once, to put them back on then." He added: "They are having their lunch break in the Queens Head over the road. Best of luck." He then walked hurriedly away towards the coal stage to survey the damage.

James hastily made his way to the pub in Great Knollys Street. He opened the door to the public bar and saw the group of mechanics enjoying their lunch. The smell of cooked food and beer made him envious, but the deed had to be done.

He called out to get their attention, trying to absolve himself of the blame. "Sorry lads but the foreman wants you back to the shed quick, because there are a few wagons off the line by the coal stage."

With the groans of annoyance sounding in his ears he beat a hasty retreat. Making his way back to the shed he knew it was fast approaching 1.30pm the time to clock off duty. When he got back to the coal stage his relief fireman was already there so he hastily picked up his lunch bag and made a fast exit before the fitters arrived. He went home with dread in his heart knowing that tomorrow he would be the butt of everybody's fun. Old-hand fireman fucking up his shift. But it didn't happen. Everybody, including the foreman, made light of the incident. The thought was that everybody can make a mistake and Ron Fry did the same thing with a 2200 engine a few months later.

DERAILMENT BLUES 1959

It was a bright sunny Sunday morning, the sky was a hazy blue with a few small clouds floating lazily by high above him. The warm morning air felt refreshing as he rode his new motorbike along the Oxford Road. He had been able to purchase a better machine, bigger and more powerful than his 350cc Ariel. The 500cc BSA A7 twin engine purred with power as he twisted the throttle to make the machine gain speed. Didn't want to be late on a Sunday he thought, the money is too handy. Sunday shifts were double pay and he speculated that his shoebox needed a boost. It had become slightly emptier after buying the big motorbike.

After parking the big shiny red and black bike in the bike shed, he stood and admired it. With the extra money from today I might be able to get some silver crash bars for it, he thought. With this in mind he booked on duty, the time was 6.30am. The engine he had to prepare was 6350 a Mogul type engine. He liked these types of engines. They were bigger than the 2200 class but not as big as the 2800 class. Something in between. A nice engine to fire and the footplate was open and comfortable, just right for this spring morning.

Just after he had collected the lamps from the lamp house his driver Bert Little arrived. Bert was a small man with a friendly open face. He smiled at James as he climbed aboard the footplate. He greeted James with a cheery voice: "Morning mate. Are you ready for a good day today? Weather's with us, isn't it?"
"Morning Bert. Yeah, the weather's fine. Might even get a sun tan," replied James with a grin.

They prepared the engine and after making the customary can of tea, ran the engine to the west Reading goods yard. Here they were backed onto a long train of low wagons that contained rails with the wooden sleeper attached. These were piled high on the low wagons, at least 4 to 5 foot high. The job for today was to transport the rails and sleepers to Theale. The line maintenance crew were to lay a new stretch of rails and remove the old stretch. The job for James and Bert was easy. All they had to do was move the wagons when required by the maintenance crew.

James lowered the firebox flap and checked that the fire was burning bright. The steam pressure was 190psi and the water gauge glass showed three quarters full. He waited for the guard to climb into his brake van and said to Bert: "All clear to go mate. Guard's in the van."
Bert moved the gear lever into full forward motion and opened the vacuum brake ejector. When the brake gauge needles registered 21 inches of vacuum he lifted the regulator. The 6350 steam engine moved forward with a loud blast of steam and smoke from the chimney. The signal man set the tracks towards Reading West Station and as they passed over the Oxford Road Bridge James looked at the road devoid of traffic on an early Sunday morning. With the heavy wagons rattling along behind them they were soon into Theale Station. The rest of the morning passed quietly as they had little to do but move the wagons now and again as requested.

At 12pm the maintenance crew announced that the work was complete and the wagons were loaded with the old rails and sleepers. The next job was to transport the old rails to Taplow goods yard, which was next to Taplow Station. The run to Taplow was made at a steady speed because of the lack of passenger services on a Sunday. The train ran into Taplow on the up relief line and the signalman had to set the line for them to cross over all three main lines to access the goods yard. This was on the other side of the station. They waited several minutes for a fast express train to clear the up main into London. The train headed by a magnificent green liveried Castle class engine roared by them at high speed, leaving a trail of smoke and steam in its wake. With the line clear the signalman set the points for the crossover. Bert set the gear lever in reverse and carefully pushed the wagons back into the yard. As they reversed into the yard the signals on the down main line were set at green for an express train.

Bert leaned over the side of the cab to watch the guard wave him gestures to push the wagons into their sidings. Suddenly Bert in a panic yelled: "THE WAGON IS FOUL OF THE MAIN LINE,"
He turned round abruptly and shouted at James: "DETONATORS!"
James threw open the tool box on the tender and grabbed the detonator canister. He leaped of the footplate clutching the canister in his right hand. With alarm he realised the danger. He saw that one of the wagons with the heavy sleepers on had tipped sideways fouling the main line. The signal on the main line was lowered giving access for an express train. He ran along the sleepers of the main line in anxious alarm, hoping the express train was some way off. He stopped at what he estimated was a quarter of a mile. He wrenched open the canister and pulled out a detonator. Bending down in distress he attached the detonator to the rail. He hurriedly ran what seemed to be half a mile and again attached a detonator to the rail. The express train was not in view yet so he continued running along the track until he was nearly into Burnham Station. Here he attached three detonators at set intervals on the track. He looked along the line and saw in alarm the front of the large steam engine heading towards him. He stepped away from the rails and stood by the side of the track. He searched in the canister to find the red flag. When he extracted it he saw in irritation that it had disintegrated into a piece of rag full of holes. Waving the ragged red flag he

anxiously awaited the engine to pull up beside him. The large Castle class engine came slowly towards him and with a loud hiss of team halted.

He looked up at the two figures on the engine towering above him. "Sorry driver, but you can't get by at Taplow, we are foul of the line," he called out to them.

The driver and fireman stared down at him and the driver replied: "We have been informed that we can go by at a slow speed, there is room to avoid the obstacle." He scowled at James and continued in a threatening tone: ""What are you buggers up to. Trying to make more overtime are we?'"

His fireman laughed and spoke to the dismayed James. "Take no notice mate. He is upset because we lose money if we are late, it's a bonus if we are on time."

The irate driver spoke again. "Do you want a ride back, and are you picking up your detonators?"

James climbed up on the big engine's footplate. As he got into the cab he said: "Thanks for the ride but you can run over the detonators, I am not bothered."

The driver opened the regulator and the engine moved forward. At once there was a loud bang, then two more. The driver stared at James and remonstrated. "Those detonators were not three yards apart, if we had been going fast it would have sounded like one!"

His fireman chuckled but said nothing. A short time later they ran over the other two detonators that exploded with loud bursts of sound. The train drew level with the wagon that was leaning dangerously close to the engine. The driver leaned out of the cab and moaned: "Bugger! You could get a bloody bus through that gap."

As they drew level with Bert sitting on the 6300 class engine, James climbed off the engine and the train continued on and moving slowly passed the wagon. James estimated the gap was not very wide, only about two-foot. If the express train had hurtled by that gap at speed, the sway of the carriages and the vibration created could have resulted in disaster. The wagon's load would have slipped and hit the train.

He walked over to Bert, who was sat on the engine, and asked: "What do we do now Bert?"

Bert gave him a cheery smile and replied: "I think a hot cup of tea would help, don't you?"

James collected the tea can and hurried across to the signal box. Inside were several people dressed in dark suits gazing at the offending wagon. As he walked in the signalman said: "Blimey mate. You were quick I didn't see you go."

James replied with self-esteem: "No, I went down that main line like a frightened rabbit, I don't think a greyhound would have caught me."

He laughed and quickly made the brew, much needed to calm his and Bert's nerves.

With the hot tea can firmly clutched in his right hand he climbed back onto the footplate. As they sat drinking the welcome brew Bert said: "You did well mate. I didn't know if you knew what to do in that situation."

James' mind went back to the interview he had with the shed clerk, when he was promoted to the position as fireman. "Yes I knew what to do but I have never done it before, and I hope to not have to again.

Yes, he thought, that was the one question the chief clerk had impressed upon me: Rule 55 protection of the train.

With nothing else to do in the situation they were given the signal to travel back to Reading loco depot. James was very pleased to wheel his shiny motorbike out of the bike shed and with alacrity head for home. The day started well and although there were a few hiccups, it ended well.

STOP ME AND BUY ONE

The day started bright and sunny. James pulled his big red and black 500cc motorbike out of the garden gate. He mounted the big machine and, using his right leg, he kicked the engine into life. The engine fired and a low growl of power emanated from the twin exhaust pipes. He rode out of the estate, and into the Oxford Road. Racing along the road with the wind blowing through his hair he headed for his friend's house in Sherwood Street. Bob Brazell, his railway fireman mate, lived in a small shop on the corner of Little Johns Lane and Sherwood Street. James had become good friends with Bob, but he also had taken a shine to his sister. He hoped she would be at home so they would walk down the lane that led to the railway line at west Reading. Here they would chat and mess about while watching the express trains go thundering by.

As he approached the Grovelands Road School area he noticed a Wall's ice cream van pulling to a stop on the opposite side of the road. To his dismay he saw the van begin to reverse across the road in front of him. He closed the throttle and pulled in the clutch lever. Braking hard he was still heading for the van at a fast speed, and he tried to pull to the left side to avoid a collision. As he ran around the rear of the van his right foot collided with a wooden step. He heard a sickening thump and a sharp pain shot through his foot. He rode up onto the path and came to a halt as his front wheel hit a wooden fence post.
"Fuck it!" He hoped he was not injured but his foot was spurting red blood across the pavement. The driver of the van leapt out of his cab and ran to the rear of the vehicle. He looked at James and in a concerned tone said: "Are you alright, mate?" James glared at him and replied, in distress, "Does it fucking look alright? I'm bloody bleeding mate!"
The driver said: "You better come into the depot mate, and I will phone for an ambulance."
He helped James dismount from the big bike and leaned it against the fence. He helped him hop into the Wall's ice-cream depot, leaving a trail of blood behind. He hopped into the depot office and sat down in a chair by a desk. The blood from his foot dripped onto the clean shiny floor. The Wall's depot manager was not pleased. He glared at James and said acidly: "Here, put this on your foot, it's making a mess on me floor."
He offered a lint pad from a first aid box. He turned to the driver and said: "Phone for an ambulance Bert, before he bleeds to death."
What sympathy, thought James. He pulled back his sock revealing a nasty gash across the top of his foot. He applied the lint pad gently to his foot, wincing at the sight.

The driver phoned for an ambulance and he was whisked away to the Battle Hospital where the gash in his right foot was stitched. He made his way home with a heavy heart. Now I have to report sick to the loco shed he speculated. Then he thought no, Reggie his next-door neighbour could do it for him when he goes into work. He left a message for Reggie with his wife and then went and sat in the big armchair and gazed gloomily out of the window. What an accident - to be injured by a Wall's ice-cream van. Stop me and buy one! Ouch! His mates would be laughing about this one.

The gash in his foot began to heal after spending a week at home with his foot raised and rested. He reported for work the next Monday. The job was an early turn 6am start, prepare a 9400 tank engine and then spend the morning shunting the coal yard in Vastern Road area.

He awoke at 4. 30am, and got dressed sitting on the edge of the bed. His foot was still painful but he was determined to return to work and keep his shoebox filling up. He pulled on his thick woollen socks, and with difficulty tugged his heavy hobnailed army boots on as well.

His motorbike was still in the police store in Valpy Street, so he had to go to work by bus. He limped to the bus stop in the Oxford Road with his Uncle Sid, who worked in the malt rooms at Courage's beer industry. The morning was icy cold with a frost making everything white and glistening. There were about eight people huddled around the bus shelter, all chatting with their breath leaving white vapour trails in the air. James thought it funny to listen to their chat.
"Morning Flo, bloody cold init?" said one individual standing wrapped in a scarf, big overcoat and flat cap.
Flo replied: "Yeah Too cold innit? You need a good cuppa tea these morning to warm yerself."
The rest of them agreed and soon the throng was praising the benefits of hot sweet tea.
"Can't go to work without a strong cuppa tea."
This carried on until a well-lit trolleybus appeared in the distance. As it pulled into the stop, the bus queue moved restlessly aboard to savour its warm interior. James got off the bus at the Bedford Road stop and limped into Great Knollys Street and across the recreation ground to the GWR depot. By the time he had booked on his foot was aching miserably. He found the tank engine at the rear of the shed by the coal stage area. He limped to the lamp house and collected two lamps. After lighting them he placed a red shaded one on the rear of the engine and a clear one on the front. His driver came walking across to the engine while he was checking the smoke box interior. Ray Swadling was his driver today. Ray was a man of about 50 years old and was of moderate height. He watched the fireman climb down from the smoke box area with difficulty and asked: "Are you ok mate" You look like your having a problem with walking?"
James replied: "Yeah, Ray. I had a motorcycle accident last week and the injury hasn't healed properly yet. He was hoping for a sympathetic ear. He was disappointed.
"Well you better not make us late off shed, so get a move on."

With that order he went off to the store to collect his oil. Thanks Ray! James remonstrated, that's all I need. Here I am, in pain, only 16 years old and feeling totally knackered. He felt a wave of self-pity come over him. Fuck it, he agitated. It's only pain. Get on with it. He hurried to finish preparing the engine and they were off the shed at the right time, although it still did not seem to please Ray.

He continued to work the week still catching the bus, and gradually his foot hurt less. The problem now was retrieving his beloved big motorcycle from the police store. He knew the tax disc was out of date but the insurance was still in date. He hoped the police would not notice.

Saturday afternoon he plucked up courage to visit the police station in Valpy Street. He enquired at the station desk if they had a 500cc BSA A7 in their store yard. The constable looked in his log book and replied; "Yes sir, I will take you out to collect it. Is it in good condition and rideable?"
James nodded his head nervously and replied: "Yes officer. It's not damaged."
He swallowed nervously and followed the officer to the store yard. The officer opened the door to the yard and James spotted his big red and silver motorbike by a wall surrounded by pushbikes of various sizes and colours.
"That's me bike, officer," he said nervously, still hoping he would not notice the tax disc. The officer helped him to pull his motorbike out of the yard and into the road. James pulled his crash helmet over his head and adjusted his mark 8 goggles. He hurriedly kicked the engine foot start, and as the engine rumbled into life he opened the throttle and shot off down the road. He smiled to himself and thought that was luck but I better renew the tax disc next payday.

THE LAMBOURNE BRANCH WITH REGGIE

James looked at the roster board for Monday. To his surprise he was rostered to work the Lambourne branch line with Reggie, his old next-door neighbour. Reggie had helped him get employment with British Rail in 1955. James had been working the main line goods trains to Swindon and Banbury for 18 months. He had also worked the Up Fly biscuits train to Acton several times. Now at the age of 17 years he felt confident to manage all aspects of the job. So he looked forward to the change of work. The Lambourne work usually consisted of a mixture of passenger traffic and goods traffic. He felt privileged to be able to work with Reggie on this important line.

Monday morning James awoke with a startled sigh. A loud rapping sound filled his bedroom. Rubbing the sleep from his eyes he climbed out of the warm confines of his bed to find the noisy rapping sound coming from his window. He pulled the curtain back to find Reggie standing fully dressed ready for work. Seeing James pulling back the curtain he looked up at him with a grin on his wrinkled features and said: "Come on boy! Hurry up and get dressed."
James looked over at his alarm clock. The time was 4,45am. He looked back at Reggie, who was still grinning with a rolled up cigarette dangling from his lower lip.
"Fuck of Reg its only 4. 45!" he protested.

Reggie took no notice of his protest, but James said: "We are not due on until 6am."

Reggie with a cajoling reply said: "Come on, if we get to work early we will have plenty of time to prepare the engine and have a cup of tea, before we leave for Lambourne."

James closed the curtain wishing Reggie would disappear like the early morning mist. He dressed and not having time to make a cup of tea, he soon joined Reggie outside the house. Reggie was waiting for him, sitting on his old upright handlebar bike. James mounted his racing bike and together they cycled along the Oxford Road, with the early morning mist making their breath condense into small vapour clouds.

They arrived at the loco shed, and after preparing the small 9414 locomotive James sat in the cab resting. Reggie climbed up onto the footplate and looking at James asked: "Will you pack the piston valve glands?"

James stared at Reggie not believing what he had requested.

He expostulated: "Pack the bloody piston valve gland Reg?"

"Yes, pack the piston glands," Reggie replied.

"But that's a fitters job," responded James in protest.

"No it's not. It's the fireman's responsibility," said Reggie with an irritable reply. "Now go to the storeman and ask for some Kevlar packing," ordered Reggie.

James climbed off the engine and reluctantly went to the shed storeroom. He returned with the Kevlar packing material grasp tightly in his right hand. He was seething with resentment. He had the feeling Reggie was enjoying his protestations and was deliberately antagonising him He thought Reggie was applying his authority as a driver to the limit.

He collected a spanner from the engine toolbox and with the packing material shoved in his overall pocket he jumped into the pit. In a crouching movement he crawled under the engine. The heat from the firebox ash pan was hot on his back as he got near to the piston gland. He stared at the piston and noticed it had an item of metal surrounding it with four nuts holding it in place. Two on one side, and two on the other side. He was not quite sure what to do. With drops of hot water falling onto his peaked cap and the hot metal burning his hand, he unscrewed the gland retaining nuts. With the gland released he pulled it back from its closed position He withdrew the packing material from his pocket. It was in the form of a piece of rope, so he wrapped it around the hot piston and pushed the metal retaining gland back into place. He screwed the four nuts up tight. Satisfied it all looked OK, he crawled back out of the hot dark confines of the engine underbelly. As he climbed back onto the footplate he saw Reggie sitting there with a tea can in his hand.

Looking at James through rheumy eyes he said: "How about making a nice can of tea?"

Still fuming with indignation James snatched the can from his hands and after climbing back off the footplate, he hurried to the drivers' cabin. He filled the can with boiling water and by now his own boiling point had reduced to a simmer.

Now his temper cooling he returned to the engine and smiling at Reggie he said: "Tea's made, you old sod."
Reggie smiled back at him and they sat drinking the hot sweet tea in a mutual truce.

They moved out of the shed onto the out going line at Reading west junction. The journey to Newbury with the little engine did not take long and at 7am they backed onto the passenger carriages in the Newbury Station platform. James jumped in between the engine and the carriage. Reggie opened the regulator and squeezed the engine and carriage buffers up tight. James lifted the big heavy engine coupling onto the carriage hook. It hung loose. Kneeling down he then shouted to Reggie: "EASE AWAY!"
Reggie released the engine brake and as the tension on the buffers eased the big coupling link snapped tight. He coupled up the vacuum brake rubber pipes and the steam heating pipes. He then climbed back onto the platform. He stepped onto the footplate and announced to Reggie: "Everything in order Reg."
He tapped open the steam heating valve handle and soon wisps of steam leaked out along the two carriages mingling with the morning mists. The signal dropped several minutes later and with a jerk the little train moved out of the station, onto the Lambourne branch line. The signalman handed the branch single line staff token to them as they passed the signal box. No train was allowed over the single line without the staff as it retained the key to open the points along the route. James fired the engine with a number of shovels full of coal as they ascended the rising line towards Stockcross and Bagnor. The water gauge glass stayed steady at three quarters full. James was enjoying the country scenery as they ran along the line at a good pace.

The mists had evaporated under the warm morning sun, and the trees and fields were a verdant green. They did not have many passengers, just a few for the racing stables at Lambourne. A few got off at the various little platforms as they stopped at them. As the train approached Eastbury, Reggie gave a toot on the whistle. He turned to James and said: "Give Eastbury Liz a wave,"
James responded: "Who the hell is Eastbury Liz?"
Reggie said, with a laugh, "Liz lives in one of the cottages over there, she loves it if we sound the whistle and wave to her."
James gazed out over the side of the engine. In the distance he could see a few cottages and he gave a casual wave. He could not see any Eastbury Liz, but hoped she was real, and saw the casual gesture.

They were soon passing Bockhampton crossing. The gates had been opened by a woman, who waved to them as they passed by. The little train then ran into Lambourne Station and came to a halt. The engine was uncoupled and after traversing the rail points recoupled on the other end of the train, ready to return to Newbury.

Reggie stepped off the engine onto the station platform. Turning to James he said: "I am going over to see the signalman and make a can of tea. Are you coming with me? I will not be back for a while?"
We like to have a chat and sometimes his daughter would be with him.

James shook his head. "No thanks. I think I will sit here and enjoy a bit of this lovely sunshine, I might even get a tan."

Reggie sauntered off towards the signal box and James settled himself on the hard wooden seat in the cab. The warm sunshine made him doze, and with the smell of coal smoke and hot oil in his nostrils he fell asleep. Reggie returned sometime later. He climbed onto the footplate and roughly shook his shoulder saying: "Come on stir yourself we are due to leave, you better make sure we are ready."

A few minutes later the signal dropped and the guard jumped into his compartment. As it pulled away from the station the little engine responded with a loud bark of steam and smoke from the chimney. The train was soon speeding through the crossing gates at Bockhamton Crossing and after another wave from the gatekeeper they were running towards Eastbury Station.

Reggie suddenly said with a sound of alarm in his voice: "Have you got the staff?"

James replied with a worried query: "No I thought you picked it up!"

Reggie now had a very worried frown on his wrinkled face. He spluttered: "Why the fuck did you forget to collect it from the signalman?"

His fireman bristled replying: "Reggie I wasn't the one drinking tea in the bloody signal box, you should have picked it up!"

The train ran into Eastbury Station with two very worried enginemen on board. As the train came to a halt a member of staff hurried along the platform, and leaning into the cab said with a laugh: "The signalman at Lambourne is not very happy with you two clowns, he's pedalling his old bike along the lane trying to catch you up."

After waiting in the little station for a short while, the figure of a hot sweating signalman, on his old bike came puffing along the lane. When he reached the platform entrance he wearily climbed off his bike and leaned it against the fence. He trudged along the platform with the staff looped around his shoulder, and as he got nearer the engine he exploded into a tirade of bad language. "Why did you forget the fucking staff Reg? Fuck me I've been chasing along them bloody lanes trying to catch you up and I swear I could have had a fucking heart attack."

With his face red with frustration he handed them the staff. He then hurried back to his bike and rode off still bristling with temper. Reggie released the brakes, and with the staff token safely on board, they continued on their way. The rest of the journey was a normal peaceful run into Newbury.

The next day they were again rostered to work on the Lambourne line. This day they pulled a small goods train along the branch line to Lambourne. The weather was fine and the sun shone bright in the blue sky, with a few cumulus clouds now and again casting shadows across the countryside. With the engine steaming well, James sat leaning over the side of the cab. He was surveying the local scenery and admiring the summer colours as the trees and fields passed by. Looking to the front of the engine he spotted a dead chicken lying beside the rails. He stared down at it as they passed by. Reggie had also seen the chicken and turning to James with a look of pleasure on his wrinkled face he asked: "On the way back from Lambourne can you jump off and get that chicken. I can have that for Sunday dinner."

James nodded a reluctant agreement, but he was not keen on the idea of leaping from the moving train to pick up a bloody chicken.

They ran into Lambourne Station and after shunting the few wagons into the sidings made the usual can of hot tea. Reggie mentioned the dead chicken to their guard telling him of their plan. "We will slow down when we get near the chicken, and my fireman will jump off and pick it up," he said with the vision of a nice dinner in his mind.

The guard told him that there was a chicken farm beside the rails at that point. Occasionally the residents strayed onto the rails with fatal consequences. Making sure the staff token was this time not forgotten they made ready to leave Lambourne at the time allocated to them. As the little goods train rattled along the branch line the occupants stared ahead getting ready to accomplish the hazardous plan. The site of the dead chicken came into sight and as they drew near Reggie applied the brakes, slowing them down to a crawl. James climbed down the side of the engine hanging on the handrail. He jumped onto the ground and running along the side of the train scooped up the chicken and threw it up on the footplate.

As he climbed back into the cab a mess of feathers, and masses of white and yellow maggots filled his vision. With a putrid smell filling his nostrils he surveyed the mess and said in disgust: "Fucking hell Reg, it's bloody rotten, I am going to sling it into the firebox."

Reggie shook his head saying, "No don't do that."

James then suspected another plan must have been formulating in Reggie's warped humorous mind.

Reggie spoke again: "When we get to Newbury we will ask the guard if he would like a nice fat chicken, then you can chuck it into his brake van."

He tittered with glee thinking of the mess that would erupt in the warm confines of the brake van. James was in complete disagreement but he knew that if he did not carry out the deed Reggie would make his life a misery for the rest of the week.

When they arrived in the Newbury goods yard James picked up the putrid chicken carcass. He climbed down the side of the engine, and walked casually back to the brake van in his right hand he held the rotten chicken, by its legs. He called out to the guard who was still sitting in the brake vans interior.

"Hey mate would you like that chicken I picked up? Reggie's not too fussy about it."

The van's door opened and the guard stepped out onto the van's veranda. The poor guard responded with a smile of pleasure on his face: "That's very nice of Reg. I can have it for dinner tomorrow."

James threw the chicken carcass onto the van's veranda, making sure it missed the doorway to the interior. It exploded in a mass of feathers and maggots. James ran back to the engine in hurry, to escape the guard's wrath. The sounds of bad language echoed in his ears as he climbed back onto the engine. Reggie sat convulsed in laughter, his watery eyes filled with tears.

That was the last time James worked the Lambourne branch line as it was closed in 1960 by the infamous Dr Beeching, while the MP Ernest Marples concentrated on building the M1 motorway.

FOGGY DAYS AND FOGGY NIGHTS

The months seemed to pass quickly as James became more skilled in the firing of different locomotives. His confidence was building, and at the age of 17 he considered himself ready to tackle any job. But the fog that began to shroud the railways in the November of 1957 created a problem. Apart from firing the engines he was required to assist the drivers to locate the signals in these difficult conditions.

One very foggy morning he was rostered to work with driver Joe Lee on the prestigious 7.48am Henley train. This was one of Reading's top link jobs. Many of British Rail's office staff worked in Paddington. Also many high profile people lived in the Henley area. These people worked in London and were reliant upon the train to get them to their places of work safely and on time. One such person was the famous Douglas Bader. Booking on at 4.30am he saw on the roster board that the Castle class locomotive 5076 Gladiator was their engine for the day. The engine was parked at the front of the shed on number two bay. After climbing onto the footplate he hung his coat and lunch bag up. He then walked to the lamp room and collected two lamps, these he lit and placed on the engine brackets. This morning he noted was foggier than normal, the sounds of the engines seemed muted by the fog, and as the smoke from the engines mixed with the fog it became dense and yellow.

The air smelled of smoke and sulphur making breathing unpleasant. He climbed aboard the engine again and saw that the coal tender was piled high with large lumps of coal, some spilling over onto the footplate. He removed his jacket and immediately felt the cold damp air chill his body. Opening the firebox door he felt some comfort as the warmth of the fire hit his body. It was burning well with the flames flickering an orange colour in the rear of the box. After inspecting the water gauge, he carried out his normal checks. Being finished with the checks he lifted the heavy iron pricker bar from the tender and pushed it into the firebox. As he was spreading the burning coals across the fire bars his driver Joe arrived. Joe climbed up onto the footplate and greeted James. "Morning. Bloomin' cold nasty morning today ain't it?"
He never removed his jacket but with a small shivery gesture went off to the store to collect his oil. Finished with pushing the burning coal across the fire bars, James struggled to remove the red-hot pricker bar from the firebox. Using a large ball of cotton waste he grasped the pricker at the cool end and swung it up onto the coal tender. He heaved a sigh of relief and sat down for a short rest. The fire did not take long to burn bright and James began to build a good bed of fire in the haycock design, high at the back, just inside the door, and sloping to the front. With the blower pushing the smoke up into the foggy morning air the steam pressure needle was soon rising to the 220psi mark. He opened the tender water valve and tapped open the steam valve to the injectors. He then swept the footplate clear with his hand brush. This accomplished, using the pep pipe he hosed the area with steam and water, also concentrating on the pile of coal in the tender. After shutting off the injector he climbed up onto the high mound of coal

in the tender and became busy whacking the large lumps into a descent smaller sizes. Even though the cold yellow fog whirled around him he started to sweat.

After Joe finished his oiling they reversed the engine up towards the water column. James climbed over the coal in the tender and onto the rear water tank area. He lifted open the large water tank lid. Using the long chain, Joe pulled the water column filling hose towards the tender. James grabbed hold of the chain and pulled the hose into the water tank filling point. As Joe opened the water the hose started to shiver and shake like a large live snake. James held the chain tight to stop the hose from thrashing itself loose. The cold steel chain was freezing his hands and he was relieved when the tank was full.

Tea was made and they moved out of the shed at 6.1am. The fog had not lifted but remained shrouding the scenery into grey and yellow oblivion. The big engine ploughed its way to Twyford Station. Here they were turned onto the Henley branch line, and had to run tender first through Wargrave and Shiplake stations, before arriving at Henley. As they ran tender first through Wargrave Station the cold foggy air stung their eyes and faces. The cold made James shiver as the sweat he had endured earlier turned his shirt into a damp mass. He struggled to see the signals, and was glad to hear the ATC control bell ring as they passed the distance signals. This was a sound that told them the home signal was green. The fog in this area he noticed was not any less, but was lighter than the area around Reading.

The thousands of open coal fires in the domestic houses belched smoke from their chimneys and made the fog turn into smog. If it was bad in Reading he dreaded what lay ahead in Paddington. After running through Shiplake Station, it wasn't long before Henley Station loomed out of the thick fog. The rail was set for them to run into a siding that contained eight passenger carriages. The big engine ran up to the train and Joe bought it expertly to a stop tight against the buffers. James climbed off the engine and crouching under the buffers he lifted the big engine coupling onto the carriages hook. He then coupled up the vacuum brake pipes, and the steam heating pipes. Standing on the engine he opened the steam heating valve and wisps of steam were silently issued from the train heating system, mingling with the foggy atmosphere.

Joe had applied the brake and wound on the manual tender brake. He smiled at James and said: "Right mate. Let's get into the nice warm carriage and have a little mike."
James readily agreed, as his damp clothes were very uncomfortable. He longed to dry out his clothes and get warm. Looking at his watch he saw the time was 7am. The morning sun was weakly trying to shine through the murky fog but the fog persisted and the morning light was grey and cold. James filled the boiler until the water gauge showed a nearly full glass. He shut the firebox dampers to help cool the firebox. He then climbed into the warm carriage. Lazing in the warm carriage he dozed. With his clothes steadily drying he felt more comfortable. The time seemed to pass to fast, and with a start he was awoken by Joe who said: "Time to put the train into the station platform, mate, so wakey wakey."

The train was pulled out of the sidings, and pushed into the platform. The train began to fill with passengers. They came hurrying along the platform choosing their favourite carriage compartments. Most were wearing heavy black overcoats and bowler hats. Some were carrying brief cases and rolled umbrellas. One tall young man, wearing spectacles, approached the engine. He stood there in the damp fog, admiring the big engine. He turned towards James, who was nonchalantly leaning over the side of the cab, and said: "You have a very good engine today."

James looked at him, and with a disdainful tone in his voice, replied: "Have we? Good. This should be an easy run today then."

He turned to Joe and nodding towards the young chap, he mouthed silently, "What does he know?"

Joe smiled and replied: "You would be surprised what these young chaps know, they are rail enthusiasts."

The young man had gone back to the train and entered the first compartment. James realised he was about the same age as himself, but he had the responsibility of getting him to Paddington safe on this horrible foggy morning.

The signal dropped with a rattle. James strained his eyes to look towards the rear of the train. The blurry figure of the guard waved his green flag and with the faint sound of his whistle sounding in his ears, he turned to Joe saying: "Right away mate."

Joe opened the regulator gently, allowing the engine to slowly move forward without the big wheels slipping. James dropped the firebox flap and threw six shovels full of coal onto the orange fire. The fire lit up the cab, throwing shadows of the two enginemen onto the fog above it. They gathered speed as the big engine pulled the train effortless along the foggy track.

Shiplake Station was soon looming out of the gloom. They ran into the station, stopping at the platform end. More passengers climbed into the carriage compartments. The same thing happened at Twyford and Maidenhead. From Maidenhead the train was non-stop into Paddington. The fog was still thick and as they ran through the Slough, the acrid smell of factory emissions was a choking concoction of chemicals and soot. The air smelled of paint fumes, James thought. Not at all pleasant.

The big engine was now travelling at an exhilarating, fast speed with the trailing smoke beating down behind. James dropped the firebox flap and shovelled coal into the white-hot glow. This illuminated himself and the footplate. The fire made his features appear red with exertion. But he found the engine was responding well to his steady firing method. They thundered through West Drayton, and Hayes with the footplate steadily vibrating. Southall Station flashed by and soon they were running through Ealing Broadway, with the fog turning to smog, the further they ran into the London suburbs.

Joe closed the regulator as they ran through Westbourne Park Station and began to apply the brakes. The train ran into Paddington, along platform 5. It slowed steadily and Joe expertly brought it to a stop just in front of the buffer board. With the water injector running, James filled the tin bucket with water. As he washed the grime from his hands he watched the passenger getting off the train and rush to the station exits.

One gentleman carrying a brief case and wearing a bowler hat called out to them, "Thank you for a safe journey." After saying this he hurried of into the fog in the direction of Praed Street. Several other passengers thanked them. Joe smiled at James saying: "Well, that's a first, never been thanked before, must be the weather."
The engine was uncoupled from the train, and as the train was removed, they followed it tender first to the end of the platform.

The signal dropped and they were given the line into the engine yard at Ranelagh Bridge. As they ran into the yard James surveyed the grimy tenement blocks that towered over them. Through the fog he saw that the walls and windows were covered in grime. The red brickwork looked dark, and some windows had tattered curtains dangling inside.

As he looked at the buildings he shuddered thinking, how can people endure living in these conditions? Compared to the clean environments of Reading this place looked Dickensian. He would not have been surprised if Fagin and his bunch of boy pickpockets had not leaned out of the windows waving to him

After turning the engine on the turntable Joe went off to make a well-earned can of hot tea. James looked at the other steam engines in the yard. They were there ready to go back into Paddington, and pull the express trains to Wales and Plymouth. They looked resplendent in their green shiny livery. With chimney copper tops and safety valve covers gleaming through the dense fog. They waited like tense animals to be fed coal and water before performing their mad dashes across the country.

As he was deep in his dreamy thoughts Joe came back with their sustenance. Hot, steamy, sweet tea. After chewing on a cheese and pickle sandwich, and consuming the tea, they vacated the yard and were directed to Acton goods yard. Here they were coupled to a long goods train to be delivered to Reading East Goods depot. The fog was as dense and yellow as earlier with no clearance likely. James realised how bad this type of fog was to your health. He knew that thousands of people had died in 1952 choking on the sulphurous soup.

The signal was given to leave the yard and they were directed onto the down relief line. Ploughing through the murky fog James leaned over the side of the cab. His tired eyes were streaming with tears as the cold air stung his pupils. Joe drove the engine steadily onward, appearing oblivious to the adverse conditions. Joe was a very stoic individual. Nothing seemed too difficult for his genial nature. James climbed back into the engine's warm cab. Pretending the fire needed his prompt attention; he dropped the flap and began shovelling coal into the firebox. The big engine pulled the goods train with ease and they ran into Reading East goods yard at12.30pm. The train was uncoupled and the engine taken to Reading loco depot to be readied for the next day. After booking off duty James wheeled his motorbike from the bike shed and rode it home with the satisfaction of knowing he had managed the 7.48 Henley train successfully.

Later that week James was rostered to work a goods train to Swindon. The train was to leave Reading West goods yard. A nice easy job with the opportunity of making some overtime he thought. His driver for that day was Alan Mccrohan. James was pleased with that because he liked working with Alan. The weather that week had been bad with thick fog casting a cloud of murkiness across the country. A driver, Bert Dobson, approached Alan and asked him nervously if he would swap turns with him. Alan cheerfully agreed. Bert's turn was an Acton run, and Bert knew the fog in London would be a horrendous obscurity.

The London fog mixed with the soot and smoke from thousands of chimneys produced the deadly smog. After booking on duty the next day James was surprised to see Bert climb onto the 2800 class engine as he prepared it. Bert explained to James the reason he was his driver for the day, admitting that he was nervous of the foggy conditions. James had never fired to Bert but he soon became comfortable with him. One of Bert's hobbies was trying to learn Esperanto, the universal language. The reason for this artificial language was to make it easier for people to converse throughout the world. It never caught on.

After preparing the engine they ran out to the exit signal at Reading West junction signal box. They ran into the goods yard and the guard coupled them up to a long train of goods wagons. The big 2800 class engine would make the job easy thought James, as he shovelled six loads of coal into the firebox. He was firing the engine with the favourite haycock method, and the steam gauge was responding perfectly, rising to 220psi. The guard went back to his brake van and Bert lifted the regulator. The engine pulled the train slowly to the signal post at Scours Lane, as they neared it the signal dropped giving them access to the main relief line. Bert looked fixedly into the murky fog straining his eyes to locate the signals. As they passed through Tilehurst Station the train picked up speed and it passed Pangbourne, rattling along at a brisk rate. The ATC bell rang as the signals loomed out of the fog. This made it easier for the driver as he knew that if the ATC bell rang the next signal would be green. All the way to Didcot the line was clear and they made good time. As the train was diverted onto the Swindon main line the ATC gave a warning whoop sound, meaning the next signal would be red. Bert looked at James with a frown of dismay. He said in a distressed voice: "I won't be able to see the next signal, its so fucking murky, can you stand on the front of the engine and tell me when you spot it?"
James looked at Bert and with an anxious tone he asked: "Stand on the front, are you joking?"
Bert said again: "No. It's no bloody joke. I can't see sod all with the fog like this!"
A sound of panic came into his voice. James, with great reluctance climbed out of the cab, and standing precariously on the small ledge inched his way onto the side of the engine. As he climbed up onto the side of the boiler, the biting cold damp air made him shudder. Hanging on desperately to the handrail, he inched his way to the front of the smoke box. As the rails and sleepers ran by under the engine he winced at the thought of falling. Standing on the front he stared into the murk and the signal emerged showing a green light. James waved his hand to

Bert shouting "SIGNAL GREEN!" Then he carefully but hastily made his way back to the warm cab. The signal sent them into Steventon loop line, safely off the main line. Bert heaved a sigh of relief, and as they slowly ran along the line towards Wantage Road Station. The rest of the trip was undertaken without Bert becoming alarmed about the fog. But when the train arrived in Swindon goods yard he hastily made his way to the station determined not to work a train back to Reading.

WRONG TRAIN

James was scheduled to work with Joe Lee. He had worked with Joe before and liked Joe's genial laid-back nature. Joe was a very experienced driver and was liked and respected by all the staff at Reading loco depot. He was pleased to see on the roster board that they were booked on the 10pm up fly train to Acton yard. The train consisted of various goods wagons that were delivered to station yards on the way to Acton. The engine they had was 6101 a Prairie tank loco. The night they booked on duty was chilly with the threat of rain in the atmosphere. So the tank engine was welcome as it provided some considerable shelter from the weather conditions. The engine was waiting on line three and had been prepared for them. James arrived early for work as usual and was putting his coat and lunch bag into the steel locker in the cab, when Joe arrived: "Hiya Sno are you ready for a quiet night? 'Cos I am."
He greeted James with a grin. Why Joe called him Sno he didn't know, but reckoned it was his own secret, because he said it with a nasal tone and always chuckled. They made the usual can of hot tea and moved the engine up to the exit signal at the east end of the shed.
Here they were given access to drive through Reading Station and back onto the goods train. When the guard had climbed onto the brake van the signal dropped. With the green light shining through the dark Joe opened the regulator and they moved onward. James fired the engine lightly because the train was not heavy and Joe used the regulator sparingly. The first stop was into Twyford yard. Here they dropped off several wagons and the next stop was Maidenhead. James was enjoying the freedom of not being under pressure. He spent time leaning out the cab and watching the lights in the windows of the houses and cottages lining the railway. The night was dark with clouds obscuring the moon and a scattering of light rain. Being in the warm cab the weather was not a bother. The stop at Slough was quickly dealt with and after a few wagons were dropped off at Drayton they ran into Acton yard where the train terminated. The time was 1.45am and they were put into a siding to wait for a morning train to be assembled for the run back to Reading.

Joe peered at James and announced: "Time for a little snooze I think," and, pulling his cap over his eyes, nodded off. James adjusted the shovel as a back prop and fell asleep himself. This was the usual easy trip James had with Joe, nice and steady, without stress. The time to collect the morning train seemed to come around too fast, as the shunters rapped on the cab doors to arouse them. They backed onto the goods train in the yard and were given the signal to leave. The run back to Reading was soon accomplished. They were able to run nonstop on the down relief line to Reading, as the traffic was light in the early hours. They arrived into Reading east yard and got relief at 6.30am.

It was March 1959 when James was to work with Joe again. It was a mild March spring day. The task today said Joe was to travel to Swindon and relieve a train coming from Severn Tunnel Junction. Nice easy job thought James. Together they walked through the shed premises toward Reading Station. As they ambled along past Reading West Main signal box they saw the familiar figure of a small Welsh fireman, Alfie Broome, walking towards them. Alfie lodged in the Didcot hostel and travelled to Reading every day for work.

Joe called out: "Hi Alfie! When is the next train to Swindon due?"
Alfie looked at his watch, and in a broad Welsh accent shouted to Joe: "If you hurry the next train on platform 4 will be for Swindon."
Joe shouted back: "Thanks Alfie. See you later."
The two of them hurried along the trackside to the station just in time to see the train pull into the station. They ran up the platform and jumped into the first empty coach. Panting, they settled down in the comfortable soft seats. "Phew," gasped Joe, "'We only just made it, didn't we?" He smiled and continued: "Now we should get there in plenty of time with this train."
They both sat and viewed the scenery as the train pulled out of the station. The train accelerated rapidly and Didcot Station was just a blur as the train ran through it heading towards Swindon. As the train ran past Shrivenham Station they prepared themselves to get off at Swindon. The train did not slow as it headed into Swindon and the two of them stared in dismay as it thundered through the station.
Joe looked at James and exclaimed: "That bloody Alfie Broome put us on the wrong train."
He started to walk into the coach corridor saying: "I better find the guard and ask him where we stop next."
Joe disappeared, going along the corridor searching for the guard. He came back ten minutes later with a look of consternation on his face. "The next stop is Swansea, the controller won't be pleased."
He sat down and smiled, the hilarity of the situation dawning on him. The train raced through the Severn Tunnel and emerged the other side into Wales. They were soon running into Swansea Station and the two enginemen, feeling desperately foolish, had to report to the control office that they had arrived - but not at the required destination. Joe went to the porter's room and made the phone call. James sat on a bench and waited for him to return. Joe came ambling back grinning. "They are OK," he announced. " Well Sno, I am off to do some shopping. Might as well make use of our mess up. I am going into Litttlewoods and buy something for my new baby daughter."

Joe sauntered off into the town centre. James sat on the station bench reading a newspaper that he had found abandoned there. When Joe returned they waited for the next train that stopped in Reading. The ride into Reading was comfortable and Joe went home a happy man clutching a bag of goodies for his baby.

THE FLAT TYRE

The day was bright with a few clouds floating about, obscuring the sun now and again. James and Joe were scheduled to work the up line pilot turn in Reading Station. The job today was to shunt the passenger and parcel coaches around the station as required. Also if an engine on a passenger train developed a fault, they were to change engines or work the train forward to Paddington themselves. After booking on duty they walked to the station to relieve the crew who had worked the morning shift.

When they arrived at the station they went to platform 2. The engine was standing in the centre bay platform. As they climbed onto the footplate to change crews the driver commented there was a slight fault to the engine. The engine was a 4986 Aston Hall. He told Joe that one of the wheels had a flat area on it. This he explained made it a bit uncomfortable when moving around the station doing the shunting duties, because the footplate vibrated a bit each time the flat area hit the rail. The engine had probably been working where there were a lot of gradients. These caused the engines to slip along the rails sometimes resulting in the flat spot.

After the change over had been completed Joe remarked: "You know what Sno, if we have to pull a passenger train to Paddington, it will have to be bloomin' slow 'cos this old engine will fall to pieces."

James agreed and as they made a few shunting manoeuvres later, he noticed how bad the engine vibrated and hoped the likelihood would not arise. But luck was not on their side. Half an hour later, at 3.30pm shunter Bob Tanner sauntered up to the engine and with a smile on his face said: "There is an express train just come into platform 2, it has a Hymek Diesel on the front and the driver said he has lost the hydraulic transmission, it can't move."

Joe and James stared at him in dismay. "You got to be joking, aren't you Bob?" Joe replied in an appealing tone.

Bob shook his head and answered in an enthusiastic manner: "Signalman will set the points for you in a minute, when you get over there I will couple you on." With the bad news imparted he walked back to the stricken diesel train.

Joe looked at James and said in a subdued voice: "We will have to take it steady with this engine, it's not going to be a pleasant ride."

James nodded agreement and began to shovel more coal into the firebox. He piled the coal into the rear of the firebox building his favourite haycock shaped fire. The steam pressure began to rise to 220psi as the dark smoke gushed from the chimney. The points were set and Joe moved the engine onto the diesel's front buffers. The shunter, Bob, jumped in between the engine and the diesel and coupled them on.

The signal to depart had fallen and looking back at the guard James saw him wave his green flag. James pulled on the whistle chain to acknowledge the guard's gesture. Joe lifted the regulator gently allowing the train to move forward slowly. It gathered speed as it passed the gasometers at East Reading. The thumping of the flat wheel became more apparent as they accelerated through the Sonning Cutting. Joe and James were both feeling nervous as the vibration increased.

All of a sudden a loud roar erupted behind them. They both looked back over the coal tender to see the diesel driver high in his cab give a two thumbs gesture to them. Then the engine began to accelerate rapidly, making the thumping vibration increase to an alarming rate. The diesel driver had regained the diesel's hydraulic transmission and was now pushing them towards Paddington at breakneck speed. The vibration was like an earthquake. The coal in the tender was being shaken onto the footplate like an avalanche. James opened the water to the injector and opened the steam valve. He desperately hosed the coal tender to try to alleviate the dust. But the vibration created more coal dust that stung his eyes and blackened his face.

Joe was staring intently in front of the engine, but the control of their speed was in the hands of the diesel driver who seemed intent on making up lost time. They went past Maidenhead in a flash of dust and smoke as James was frantically trying to fire the engine and keep his balance. Joe dashed across to his side of the cab as they thundered through Burnham, muttering: "I think there is a speed check at Slough." He craned his neck over the side of the cab.

Slough Station passed in a blur of coal dust and asbestos. No check board was seen. The engine was thumping and vibrating so violently that asbestos dust was now shaking out of the firebox covers. The coal was still falling onto the footplate and James was still brushing it back, determined to keep it from becoming a tripping hazard. Looking back at the two enginemen sat up high on the diesel he noted with irritation that they were laughing at their plight. To them sat in their comfortable warm cab it all seemed hilarious. James stopped firing the engine after they thundered through Southall Station. The barrage of vibration and noise was becoming more intense as the engine was pushed through Ealing Broadway He realised that the engine was not burning the coal very fast because they were being pushed. So he sat down and rubbed the coal dust from his eyes and face. The train passed through Westbourne Park Station and started to slow as it approached Paddington Station

The train ran slowly into Paddington Station, and when they stopped the fireman on the diesel climbed down from the cab. He walked over to the steam engine. Joe and James were using a bucket of hot water to wash the grime from their faces, each of them looked like blackened coal miners. The neat clean fireman grinned and said: "I will uncouple for you mate, you look a bit dishevelled."

James thought of many harsh replies but said nothing. He was only glad that the horrific ride was over, and was thankful for the help offered. When the diesel and train coaches were removed from the platform and transported to Old Oak Common depot, the engine had to be driven back to Reading loco shed. Joe and his dishevelled fireman accomplished that task at a much slower speed. When they arrived at Reading they left the engine standing on the coal stage. They were both content to see the last of it. James was only to glad that the day was over. He hoped that he would never have to repeat a journey like that again.

OLLIE STANNET AND THE DOUBLE TRIP

The early morning sun shone through the bedroom curtains making the bedroom warm and light. The alarm clock rang loud in his ear, awaking him with a start. James wearily reached out an arm and shut off the offending noise. He rubbed his eyes to clear his vision and swung his legs out of the bed sheets to sit on the bedside. He dressed himself in a tee shirt and boxer shorts. He then put on a blue denim shirt and denim jeans. He pulled on a thick pair of woollen socks.

Already, as he dressed he was feeling the heat of the summer morning. As he continued putting on his overalls and heavy boots he thought to himself today might be pleasant to laze about. But working on a hot steam engine it is going to be a nightmare. Today he was rostered to work with driver Ollie Stannet. Ollie was a stout man aged about 50 with dark features. He was a very experienced driver and worked on the more senior shifts at Reading. The job they were to work today was Reading to Paddington with a 6100 Prairie tank locomotive. The number of carriages was normally six and they had to stop at every station.

James had never worked on these trips before and was somewhat tense. He hoped he would be able to manage the task without mishaps. He went into the kitchen and made a hot cup of tea. But as he drank the tea he began to perspire. The hot tea made him feel refreshed but not any cooler. The ride to work on his motorbike with the morning air blowing in his face was a welcome boost to his confidence. Arriving at the loco depot he felt more relaxed.

He viewed the roster board and saw that their engine for today was a Prairie tank 6156. It was standing on number two line outside the shed. He was pleased to find it had already been prepared. As he was walking out of the office area Ollie arrived. He smiled at James and said with a cheerful voice: "Morning mate. Looks like we are going to have nice day today."
He was gazing up at the blue sky as he spoke.
"It's a nice morning, but a bit warm for working on these tank engines," replied James.

They both climbed up into the warm cab. James noticed how clean and tidy the cab was. It had been prepared with professional competence and he admired the way the fireman had left it so tidy. He removed his jacket and hung it up in the corner of the cab. He then rolled up his overall jacket sleeves. That felt a lot cooler he thought to himself. After making a can of hot sweet tea they prepared to leave the shed. James set the points to the outgoing line and he clambered on the engine as Ollie moved up to the outgoing signal post. James opened the firebox door and the heat invaded the cab raising the temperature instantly. He placed a few shovels full of coal into the firebox and closed the doors to reduce the heat in the cab. The engine was facing forward towards the east. So the journey to Paddington he assumed would be pretty well dust-free. The signal dropped giving them access through the station and into the middle platform bay. Here they backed onto a train of six carriages. Ollie ran the engine onto the train's buffers and James climbed between the engine and carriage to lift the engine coupling onto the carriage hook. He then coupled up the vacuum brake pipes. He did not bother with the steam heating pipe. The train was due to leave at 7.15am. James was well prepared for the journey to start. The firebox was filled with a good bed of burning coal, and the water gauge glass was three quarters full. The steam pressure was 200psi. The train began to fill with passengers, and at the precise time of 7.15am the guard waved his green flag and gave a blast on his whistle. With the platform signal lowered Ollie opened the main brake ejector and lifted the regulator high. The train moved forward, rapidly gaining speed.

As they passed the East Reading gasometers, viewed on their right hand side, showers of smoke steam and sparks blasted from the chimney. By the time they were running through the Sonning Cutting they were traveling at a very fast rate. The engine was responding well to Ollie's heavy-handed way of driving. James wondered if Ollie was going to leave every station at such a fast rate of speed. If so then it was going to have a heavy toll on the fire bed. He would have to fire the engine little and often to keep a good level of burning coal in place.

They ran into Twyford Station with the steam gauge keeping at 220psi. The heat in the cab was increasing as James opened the firebox door to add more coal into the orange glowing mass. He was beginning to perspire heavily, with sweat running across his forehead and stinging his eyes. The guard gave them the signal to leave and Ollie once more lifted the regulator high and the train shot forward at the same fast rate of speed. This was the method of driving that Ollie used and James had to fire the engine heavily to maintain a reasonable fire bed. He was very pleased as they eventually ran into Paddington Station. Some respite at last he anticipated, but no sooner had they stopped than Ollie directed him to uncouple the engine. As the passengers were hurrying along the platform he climbed between the engine and carriage and uncoupled the train. He wearily stepped back onto the engine and Ollie moved the engine forward, descending into part of the London underground system. Here the points were set for them to run around to the other side of the train. After the movement was completed James again had to couple the engine to the train.

On the platform alongside the engine was a water column. Ollie waited for him to clamber back onto the platform. He then gestured at James to climb up onto the engines side to fill the water tanks. James wearily shook his head and ascended the engines steps onto the top of the tank. He pulled the water hose into position and watched as the cool water poured into the tank. He would have loved to dive in with it, just to cool his perspiring torso. With the tank filled and the train coupled up he sank into his wooden seat on the engine. He wiped a grubby handkerchief across his face, mopping away the sweat that ran down his forehead. He sat there watching the people scurrying about when Ollie appeared with a very welcome can of tea. They sat and drank the nectar. The sweet, moist tea eased his dry mouth and throat. "Bliss," he thought.

The time soon came for them to leave again, and Ollie with his heavy method of driving blasted them back to Reading, stopping at every station on the way. The engine was now running bunker first, this added to the discomfort, as the coal dust was blown into their face. As they raced past the east Reading gasometers, James was grateful to see Reading Station come into view. The need for a rest was paramount in his mind. Running into Reading Station's platform three, they came to a halt. Brian Revell, the station shunter, uncoupled them and after running around to the reverse end of the train they then had to manoeuvre it into the centre platform bay. Here they had to fill the water tank, ready for the return journey to Paddington. James also had to trim the coal in the coalbunker. He was now bathed in sweat. The sun was beating down relentlessly. He found that the heat and sweat was making his legs and waist sore. The denim jeans and shirt were soaked and he felt absolutely exhausted.

After another can of tea, and a cheese and pickle sandwich, the time came to repeat the journey to Paddington. To James, this job in the hot conditions was torturous. At the end of the day he was exhausted to the point of rebellion. If he had been asked to go another mile he would have asked for his P45.

The journey home on his big motorcycle was bliss as the cool rush of air chilled his sweat soaked clothes. Because of the hot sweaty work he developed a heat rash in a delicate area and had to visit his doctor. The doctor inspected the rash and commented sympathetically: "How sad, use plenty of talc next time." But he did give him some cream to ease the dreadful itch.

THE PIGEON SPECIAL

It was a sunny Saturday in April 1960. James' mate, John, was on annual leave. James was booked on a Pigeon Special train. The driver he had was Len Kilham, a burly chap in his thirties. This was the first time he had worked with Len and the train had to be relieved at Reading West Station. It had evidently started at Southampton and was to be terminated at Birmingham. James met Len in the booking office and together they sauntered along the Reading West junction line to the Reading West Station. They waited on the platform and James noted the time was 10.30am. James removed his jacket and rolled up his overall sleeves hoping to get a bit of a tan on his arms. The weather was warm for April and James revelled in the fresh spring air. One of the best things about working on steam trains he thought was the open-air life. Some drivers said their wages were poor because they enjoyed the work so much and that if it wasn't for putting food on the table they would work for nothing.

The Pigeon Special appeared in the distance and ran into the station to come to a stop with a hiss of steam from the piston glands. The two of them climbed onto the footplate asking: "Is this the Pigeon Special?"
The driver looked at them with a quizzical frown on his face and replied: "No. This is not a Pigeon Special but it is a train of RAF officers. Same thing I suppose. They all fly don't they?"
Len laughed and commented: "We were told it was a Pigeon Special, someone must be taking the micky."

The driver and fireman exchanged information and got off onto the platform. They now had a long walk to the Reading main station. With a deep satisfaction James realised the engine was a Hall class. His favourite steam engine. He noticed the coal in the tender consisted of a hard slate type coal. This type of coal burned with a good heat but burned voraciously. He thought he was going to be using the shovel much more than normal on this journey to keep the firebox full.

The signal dropped and James gazed along the platform to see the guard wave his green flag. James gave Len the tip: "Right away Len."
Len lifted the regulator gently to allow the engine to pull slowly out of the station. It gathered speed as they turned onto the branch line to Tilehurst Station. He expertly adjusted the gear handle until the steam engine was responding with a speedy acceleration and they ran through Pangbourne with James shovelling coal into the firebox with gusto. The fire burned with a vivid yellow glare. Each time he dropped the firebox flap to add more coal into the blaze the heat radiated intensely into his face. He began to perspire. The sweat running down his forehead, made him feel irritable. He mopped his brow with his grubby handkerchief and leaned over the side of the cab. The cool air rushing past his face was like a balm, drying the sweat and quenching his hot frame.

He looked at the steam pressure gauge and noticed it was falling to 200psi. He reluctantly picked up the shovel and added more coal into the firebox. The steam pressure began to rise to 225psi and the safety valve on top of the boiler started to lift. This issued a stream of steam to blow across the cab. James dropped the firebox flap allowing cool air to flow into the fire. The safety valve dosed and the waste of steam stopped. He then opened the water feed injector to raise the water level in the gauge glass. When the water feed was running he pulled the pep pipe away from the side of the cab and hosed the coal tender with steam and water to douse the coal dust. The train was now driving along at a rapid speed with Len diligently watching for the signals. They ran through Oxford Station and James was still bent over firing the engine as the firebox hungrily burned the hard slate type coal with an appetite for more.

By the time they ran into Wolverhampton Station the coal tender was depleting rapidly. The train was delayed only for a short time and once again they pulled out of the station with James shovelling the snap crackle and pop type coal with slightly less verve.
He glanced over to Len and remarked: "Bloody hell Len. This coal ain't half burning fast. I hope we will have enough to get to Birmingham!"
Len surveyed the coal tender and replied: "Yea. We will have enough 'cos we get relief at Birmingham and the engine will go to shed there."

With Len's confident words giving him assurance James continued to feed the firebox with zeal. Clouds of black smoke curled behind them as they hammered on to Birmingham. The train ran into Birmingham Station with the fire in the firebox at a low level. James realised that if the engine was going to the locomotive depot when they got relief, the fire cleaning staff would have an easier task.

Len bought the train to a steady halt at the end of the platform and all the blue uniformed pigeons disembarked. James looked around the platform for their relief crew but spied only one solitary engineman stride towards them.

He climbed onto the footplate and said with an apologetic tone in his voice: "Sorry lads. I haven't got a fireman. Are you willing to go on with me piloting you?"

Len, with some hesitation, asked: "Where does the control want us to go on to. I thought the train terminated here?"

With a sympathetic aura the driver replied: "The control staff wants you to take the train coaches back to Reading."

James gaped at the driver in dismay thinking, please say no Len. But Len being a good responsible person turned to his dismayed fireman and asked: "Are you alright to go back to Reading mate? Looks like we should have enough coal."

The burden of agreement had now been placed with James. He was loath to disappoint Len who seemed keen to agree to the request, so against his better judgement he replied: "Yeah. I am ok with that, but I just hope we have enough coal left in the tender."

With the decision to continue back to Reading made, Len said: "Right mate. Let's get into the tender and shovel all the coal forward, we will pile it up high."

The two of them clambered to the back of the pile of coal and with a pick and shovel. They excavated all of the coal from the rear of the tender. Len pushed it forward, and with a newfound vigour, James piled the coal high at the front of the tender. Panting with weariness James then had to rebuild the fire in the firebox. With the task accomplished the signal was lowered to give them the line to Stourbridge. This put them in a long curve of 12 miles and as the train passed Stourbridge it was now heading back to Reading.

At Stourbridge the relief driver climbed off the engine and Len took back control. Len knew the line from Stourbridge and informed James that there was quite a steep incline at Honeybourne. "Best you keep a good bed of fire for Honeybourne, 'cos that is a heavy old incline and I will have to give it a bit of welly to get up there."

James looked ruefully at the receding pile of coal and was perturbed to see how small it looked. "Fuck it!" he thought and began to add more coal into the fire. As they made progress towards the Honeybourne bank the engine was steaming first rate. The incline became more noticeable and Len lifted the regulator handle to gain more energy to pull the train up the slope. The chimney was blasting smoke, steam and sparks as the train careered forward. The steam pressure started to fall and the water in the gauge glass showed half full. They ran through a small tunnel and as the engine emerged from the tunnel the station came into view. Len called out to James: "Are you struggling a bit, that incline's a bastard. We usually need a banker engine to help, but we made it didn't we?"

James surveyed the steam pressure and water level, and turned to Len to complain: "Yeah Len I am struggling now, but the coal we have left is of a better quality, it don't burn so fast, but it gives less heat, a lot of it is dust."

Len had now shut the regulator and, as the train ran into the platform, he replied: "I will tell the signalman that we need water, so when the tank is filling it will give you time to recover."

Len ran the train to the end of the platform where a water column was positioned. He stopped opposite and then called out to the signal box telling the signalman of their need for water. James climbed over the small pile of coal to the back of the tender. He pulled the water column bag towards the tender and opened the water tank lid. With the bag placed in the tank Len opened the water valve and the tank began to fill. James climbed back onto the footplate and shovelled more coal into the fire. The steam pressure soon regained to 220psi and with the water injector running the boiler was filled to three quarter full. The journey to Oxford went without any problems, and the train was soon heading towards Reading. The signalman at Tilehurst sent them into the Reading West Junction goods yard. They came to a stop opposite the shunters' cabin. James looked at the small insignificant pile of coal dust in the tender. He realised It did not amount to about a sack full.

While they sat reflecting on the journey a shunter came over to them and called out: "Control wants you to take the coaches to Basingstoke."

Len and James laughed at the shunter's remark and shouted back with two words, one of them being "Off!"

Len called out: "There is no way we can go to Basingstoke, the coal tender is empty."

The shunter returned to his cabin to give the controller the bad news and James uncoupled the engine from the train. The signal dropped and with a farewell wave from the shunter they went into the loco depot. Here the engine was parked on the coal stage area. The two weary enginemen sauntered to the office and Len commented; "I reckon we have covered about two hundred and eleven miles today."

James reckoned it felt like double that, and the gripe was that they still did not make any overtime that day.

THE TROWBRIDGE BLOWBACK

The job he was booked on today was a passenger train to Trowbridge. The day was a spring day with grey clouds and a strong west wind that was fresh and cool. Just right he thought as he had to prepare a 6100 Praerie tank locomotive. The cab on these locomotives were cramped and hot in the summer so the weather conditions made for a more pleasant working day.

He climbed up into the small footplate area of the engine and began to prepare it. He noted that the water in the gauge glass showed 6 inches of water in the boiler this meant the boiler was half full.The steam pressure gauge was 160 psi.Pulling open the firebox doors he saw that the fire was glowing a bright red in the back of the grate. The heat of the fire radiated on his face as he checked the firebox for any water leaks. He then spent a good 45 minutes building the fire and tidying the cab area. He was pleased with the clean foot plate area and went to the drivers cabin to collect some old newspapers. He spread the newspapers over the rust colourd shelf at the back of the cab.The newspapers acted as a clean table cloth he mused and it made the shelf look cleaner. Better for eating your cheese and pickle sandwiches from out of your lunchbox and standing a hot can of tea on.

His driver for today was Joe Lee. Joe smiled as he saw his firemans

attempt to make the cab look tidier but never said a word.

As Joe completed his oiling routine he stood by the side of the engine and asked his fireman to drive the engine back over to the water cloumn on the opposite line. James was pleased to be trusted to drive the engine and opened the vacuum brake ejector and watched the gauge as it registered 21 inches of vacuum. This gave him a perfect brake to stop the heavy 17 ton engine on the rail that sloped downwards towards the water column. He released the brake and moved the big gear lever forward, he then lifted the steam regulator handle to admit steam to the driving cylinders.The engine responded with a sharp bark of steam and smoke from the chimney and it accelarated forward fast as it moved over the points to the water column. He applied the brakes gently as the engine moved down the slope towards the water column but the rail was wet with early morning dew. This caused the big wheels to slide on the falling gradient. The engine gaining speed slipped passed the water column and to his alarm he saw that a another 2200 class engine was parked outside the shed in front of him.He also notice there were two men sitting in the cab having a peaceful tea break. He desperatley shouted at them to release their engine brake so when he collided with them it would lessen the impact of the 17ton collision. The shouted warning did no good as both men when they realised he was not going to stop jumped off the engine. In panic James bent over and tugged at the small sand levers near the floor of the cab. This let a stream of sand from the sand boxs onto the rail. The sand appeared to do its intended work and he felt the engine come to a stop without the expected resounding crash of buffers. He stood up and looked over the side of the engine to see that he had stopped a foot or so away from the buffers of the other engine. The driver and fireman stood looking at him and shook their heads in admonishment as much as to say "You daft sod!"

Joe appeared at the side of the engine and said in a mocking voice "That was a near thing now move back to the water column mate" The shaken fireman once more put the gear lever forward and drove the engine back up the slope to the column. The tank was filled and after a hot can of tea was consumed they made their way from the shed to Reading station. Here they backed onto a train of six coaches in number one bay.

The 6100 Praerie tank locomotive steamed easily and James was content as he leaned over the side of the cab admiring the scenery as it sped by.They stopped at all the small country stations on the way to Newbury and as they passed Newbury he relished the views of the countryside. The river kennet and the kennet and avon canal ran alongside the railway as they passed Hungerford and Bedwyn. The mornig sun breaking through the clouds sparkled on the river and canal adding life to the green fields and woods at the side of the railway.

After leaving Savernake station the engine running bunker first was speeding the train towards Pewsey station when suddenly there was three loud explosions. BANG ! BANG! BANG! The sound resonated in the confined cab. This was three detonators laid on the line to warn of danger. Joe immediately applied slammed on the brake making the train to slow down rapidly. But the fire in the white hot firebox suddenly burst out into the cab in a sheet of red hot flame. It seemed the fire in the firebox was still travelling and engulfed the cab in terrifying flames. James in panic jumped to the cab doorway feeling the heat searing the backof his overall jacket. He hung over the side of the engine as Joe quickly hit the blower valve handle to send a jet of steam up the chimney. This had the affect of drawing the flames back into the firebox. James turned to see his paper table cloth on the back shelf scorched and burning. He picked up a brush and swept the paper onto the cab floor where he stamped on it to extinquish the burning material. The train had now stopped and a person walking alongside the train called out "Sorry to stop you driver we have a landslide further on, but you can proceed with caution"

Joe opened the large ejector to release the brakes and lifted the regulator handle. The train ran towards the land slip area at a slow speed. "Bloody hell mate that was a bit dodgy that bloody fire should not have done that!" said his shook up fireman. Joe smiled and commented " Yea that fire never had any brakes on it and wanted to carry on travelling by its self!" he laughed and said "Never known that to happen before"

At Pewsey they collected the single line staff token and were diverted onto the Devizes single branch line. The heat in the cab had subsided and the run accross the branch line to Devizes was a pleasant ride through the open green countryside.They stopped at Devizes and then travelled to Trowbridge station. Here there was a post beside the railway to catch the the staff token. James leaned over the side of the cab with the wind blowing in his face. He aimed the staff token hoop at the catcher post and missed it. He watched as the staff token bounced off the post and tumbled erratically onto the ground and bounce along the track. "Fuck it I have missed thecatcher mate!" he shouted to Joe. His driver laughed and said "Well the signalman will not be happy, he will have to look for it, hope it never bounced to far!"

The train ran into Trowbridge station and James watched the passengers as they climbed on and off the train. He spotted a black cat running along the platform heading his way. But the cat hopped along on three legs? He turned to Joe and said "Here Joe there`s a black cat on the platform with three legs, looks bloody funny" Joe replied "Oh yes that`s the station cat don`t know how it lost one of its front legs though" The cat sat opposite the engine and sitting on its tripod leg stared at them with its green eyes unperturbed by the noisy steam engine. James smiled at the cat and said to Joe" Are black cats supposed to be lucky mate because this one is giving me the eye?" Joe laughed again Don`t know about that mate , but he can`t be very lucky, he has lost one of his legs" James felt that the cat was a bad luck cat then and he felt uncomfortable.

The guard blew his whistle and Joe lifted the regulator and as the train moved forward James pulled on the whistle chain. The sound of the steam whistle sounded loudly but the black cat didn`t budge as they pulled out of the station. It did not seem long before they were running into Westbury station. Here they were relieved by another crew. They made their way to the porters room and brewed a can of tea. As they sat on a station bench they watched as their train to be worked back to Reading approached the station. It was a fast passenger train straight through to Reading and then London. Joe had mentioned to his fireman that it was a diesel headed train so he would be second man in the cab. The train pulled into the station and as James climbed up into the cab he looked at the clean interior and it felt strange to sit in the soft cab seats in his greasy coal stained overalls. The view out of the window was much clearer than a steam engine. There was no boiler or coal bunker to impede the view. He thought this was going to be a very good ride back to Reading.After exchanging verbal instructions from the crew they were given the signal to leave. Joe gave a blast on the horn and opened the throttle. With a roar of diesel smoke the train pulled out of the station and accelerated fast. The powerful engine roaring with sound propelled the train into a gathering speed and they were soon travelling at 70 to 80 miles per hour. James watched the scenery flashing by the window and the view forward was exhilarating. The signals were easy to see and the track clear of any incumbrance. The train thundered through Pewsey and raced towards Savernake station. As they passed Savernake there was a curve on the rail as it headed towards Hungerford.The train pulled round the curve and to Joe`s dismay an alarm bell rang in the cab. "Blimey thats a fire alarm bell!" He turned to his second man and said "Go back into the engine room and see if there is any sign of a fire!" James was startled.He did not relish going into the small confines of the engine room.But he promptly stepped across to the rear of the cab and opened the narrow door. The deafening thunderous sound of the engine only inches away from his body in the narrow passageway made him recoil. But he peered into the dark areas for any sign of fire or smoke. To his relief all was clear and he opened the narrow door to exit to the quieter area of the driving cab. "It all clear in the engine room mate but its bloody noisy, made me ears ring!" Joe nodded in acknowledgement and heaved a sigh of relief. "It must have been the vibration from the curve at Savernake that caused it to ring" he muttered. The rest of the journey into Reading was uneventful and they got relieved in the station.

As he made his way home riding his 500cc BSA motorcycle he was pleased the working day was over. He was glad to throw his dirty overalls into a pile in the laundry basket and after sitting himself comfortable in the big armchair in the warm living room fell asleep.

TED BYE AND THE 8.48

September 1961. As James was looking at the rota for the next day, which was a Friday, he saw that his driver was Ted Bye. James knew that Ted was a fireman in his late twenties. Although he must have been a passed fireman. As a passed fireman he was allowed to act as a driver if required. The pair of them were required to travel to Old Oak Common loco shed to prepare an engine and then work the 8.48 train from Paddington to Reading. The reason must have been that Old Oak Common had been short of a crew for this train. This was an unusual job for Reading men. James met Ted in the booking office at Reading loco. The time was 4.0pm with dark clouds giving a damp overcast outlook for the day.
"Hello mate are you ready for a fun day?" asked Ted with a wide grin on his face.
"I have never been to Old Oak before, its going to be a bit strange," replied James.
Ted's young features lit up as he said; "Well, I have and it's no big deal. Although it is much bigger than this depot and it's a roundhouse design with all the preparing done inside the shed."
Ted threw a big leather bag over his shoulder and together they walked to Reading Station to catch a train to Paddington. They managed to catch a fast train from platform 2 and were soon in Paddington. Now they had to get to Old Oak Common depot. The trains arriving at Paddington had their coaches taken to Old Oak Common depot sidings to be cleaned so Ted and James jumped aboard one of these to hitch a lift.

As the coaches were pulled out of Paddington James looked at the tall grimy appartments that dominated the skyline and grimaced at the sight. He had been running into Paddington on the 7.48 Henley train often and he was always mesmerised by the tall dark Victorian apartment blocks that towered over the area. The train slowed and came to a halt in the large coach sidings. Ted and James clambered off the coach and headed towards the locomotive depot. Ted was right, thought James. This place is much bigger than the Reading depot. In fact it is huge. The interior of the shed had four turntables with rails radiating out around them. He walked into the huge shed and gawped at the number of large engines parked around the turntables.

The engine they were allocated was 7013 Bristol Castle. It was on one of the rails radiating from the turntables. James climbed aboard and surveyed the footplate in the dim light, while Ted went off to the stores to collect the locker keys. When he returned they opened the locker and Ted went back to the store to collect the oil that was required to lubricate the engine.

James was totally at loss about the plan of this huge shed and was glad that Ted knew his whereabouts. James climbed up onto the front of the engine and opened the smokebox door. He inspected the interior and, satisfied it was OK, he closed the big door and turned the handles to lock it. He then placed two oil lamps on the buffer beam. Red on the front and a clear one on the rear. The reason for this was that they would be travelling tender first to Paddington. He climbed back onto the footplate and opened the firebox doors.

He saw that the fire was burning well in the rear of the box, so he lifted the long heavy pricker bar from the coal tender. He pushed it into the firebox to spread the hot burning coal across the wide interior. When he was satisfied with its spread he withdrew the red hot bar and with a struggle, trying not to burn himself, placed it back in the tender. He began to shovel more coal into the hot blazing mass. The water gauge glass showed half full and the steam pressure was rising to 160psi. The big engine was responding well thought James. He climbed off the footplate and jumped into the pit. Crouching down he crawled under the engine to inspect the ash pan. With the hot metal radiating onto his back he was pleased to see it clear of ash and clinker. The red hot fire bed glared into his eyes and sweat trickled down his back. He climbed wearily out of the pit and wiped a hand across his brow. He felt the perspiration as it ran down his forehead. Preparing steam engines in the sheds interior was too bloody hot, he speculated. Much better to be outside of this dark area.

He climbed back onto the footplate and commenced to break up the big lumps of coal with a coal pick. Then he raked it into a high stack. He finished the work by opening the water injector and washing the footplate and stack using the water pep pipe. He stood back and admired his handiwork. He was pleased it looked so clean and tidy with the cab control front and pipework glinting in the fire's glow. When Ted finished his oiling they were ready to leave the shed's domains.

The light was failing now and they backed up to the exit signal in darkness. As they were standing at the signal they heard a voice emanating from the ground area. As they both peered into the black void at the driver's side of the engine they saw a lone figure dressed in a long black raincoat and wearing a trilby hat. He looked up at them and asked in a loud voice: "Can you give me a lift to Paddington driver?"
Ted replied cautiously: "Yeah. I suppose we can, get up here mate."
The figure clambered out of the darkness and up into the illuminated cab. "Thank you driver." He politely remarked.
The signal arm dropped and Ted lifted the regulator for the engine to run back towards the station with a staccato beat from the chimney sounding loud in the dark damp air. The journey to the station came to a stop just outside the platform area. They stood at the entrance signal for several minutes and Ted peering around the incumbent figure in the black mac whispered: "Put the handbrake on mate."
James stood up from his seat and wound the tender handbrake on. The signal arm dropped and James had to release the handbrake again. He was puzzled about that.

As the engine reversed back the lighted platforms came into view and they ran into platform 2 onto an eight coach train waiting there.
Ted slowly moved the engine up to the coach's buffers and as they touched he squeezed them up tight compressing the springs.
James climbed off the engine and walked to the rear of the tender, where he climbed down from the platform to crouch under the big buffers. The figure in the big black mac followed him and stood on the platform watching intently.

James lifted the heavy coupling onto the coach hook and crouching down he shouted to Ted: "EASE AWAY!"
Ted released the brake and the compressed buffers pushed apart snapping the heavy coupling tight and rigid above his head. He continued to couple up the vacuum brake pipe and the steam heating pipe. This complete he climbed back onto the platform and, with the figure following him, climbed back on the engine. The person in the black mac stepped onto the footplate and announced in an authorised manner: "I will be riding with you to Slough, driver. I am a footplate inspector OK?"
Ted looked askance at James and replied: "That's fine with us isn't it mate?" he winked at James and grinned.
James thought: "You sneaky bastard. Why didn't he say that at Old Oak? The sneaky bastard."

James looked at the fire and saw it was blazing well in the firebox doorway. James opened the ash pan dampers wider to allow more air into the fire to assist combustion. The guard waved his green flag and Ted wound the gear handle into full forward gear. He lifted the regulator and with a loud blast of steam and smoke the big engine pulled the train out of the station.

The sounds from the loud blasts echoed around Ladbrooke Grove and Ranlagh Bridge as the train gathered speed. Ted adjusted the gear handle to set the optimum head of steam and soon they were accelerating through West Ealing. The engine vibrated gently with its pistons thrusting the big wheels turning them briskly. James moved over to the driver's side of the cab and opened the exhaust steam water injector. This used exhaust steam and filled the boiler at a slower rate but did not draw down the live steam pressure. With the injector running continuously they hammered through Southall Station at an express train rate. James fired the engine sparingly as the fast beat of the chimney was making the fire burn evenly. The hot fire burning up against the firebox flap illuminated the cab with a yellow glare. The train dashed through Iver and Langley stations and Ted now had the regulator closed. He applied the vacuum brakes gently to slow the train as it approached Sough Station. The lights of the station came into view and Ted expertly brought the train to a halt at the end of the platform. The sneaky bloody inspector stepped onto the platform and bid them goodnight. He then walked off to the station exit.

The guard waved his flag and their journey commenced again. James kept the exhaust steam injector working and the engine to his delight maintained its steam pressure at 220psi all the way towards Reading. Ted's driving skill impressed James. The journey was so comfortable that he could have gone another 38 miles easily. The train dashed through Sonning Cutting and the East Reading gasometers came into view. Ted slowed the train as it approached Reading Station. The platform sped by as the train ran into the station. James could see two persons standing at the end waiting to relieve them. The engine came to a stop and their relief crew climbed on. James spoke to the fireman saying with cheerfulness; "You have a brilliant engine here mate, no trouble at all it's a pleasure to work on."

He pick   'ed walked to the smaller loco shed to book off duty.   work was completed.

JOHNY EAGL

After spending some time working with drivers Arthur Hutchins, Alan Mccrohan, and Joe Lee, James was allocated a driver by the name of Johny Eager. James did not realise at the time that this was his nick name, not his real name. John was a man of about 5 foot 8inches of moderate stature. He was a very genial natured individual, and James was pleased to know that John was very like his previous drivers in his demeanour. John also had a slight speech impediment, in the form of a stutter. This he noticed was more evident when John was under pressure.

The first shift James worked with John was on a coal train from Basingstoke. James met John in the shed office and after booking on duty at 10pm they were instructed to prepare engine number 2847. The engine was standing at the rear of the loco shed on line 8. James meandered over to the lamp house and collected two lamps. When he arrived at the engine John was busily collecting the oil cans to go to the oil stores. The area where the big engine stood was poorly lit, so James found several flare lamps to help illuminate the footplate. He completed the preparation tasks and was busy tidying the footplate when John climbed on to fill the lubricator in the cab. James grabbed hold of the coal pick laying in the tender and climbed up onto the large pile of coal stacked high in the tender. He balanced precariously on top of the coal and began to smash the large lumps into a more manageable size. Standing on the coal heap he was chatting with John as he trimmed the coal pile.

All of a sudden the loose coal he was standing on began to slide sideways. To his bewilderment he lost his footing. He fell sideways with the coal and pitched over the side of the tender. The action to him seemed to go into slow motion. He desperately tried to grab the top of the tender side plate but only succeeded in turning himself head first towards the dark void below. With a strangled cry he hit the ground with his hands stretched out before him and rolled over onto his side. He lay on the dark damp ground dazed. John was still filling the lubricator, and seemingly chatting to James.

But when he glanced over his shoulder all he saw was a vacant heap of coal in the tender. With a look of astonishment on his face he asked: "W w-w- where are you m-m- mate?"
With a shaky distant voice emanating from the dark ground James replied: "I am down here!"
John leaned over the side of the footplate and peered into the darkness. "H-h- how the f-f-fuck did you get down there so f-f-fast?" he stuttered.
"I fell off the bloody tender, the coal slipped and I went with it," responded James. He stood up and brushed the coal from his overalls.
"Are you al-alright?" John asked him, with a concerned tone in his voice.

James grabbed hold of the handrails and hauled himself back onto the footplate. As he stood there, John peered at him and said with a chuckle; "You got a dirty chin mate, is that from the fall to the ground?"
James pulled out a grubby handkerchief from his pocket and wiped his sore chin. "Yeah. I went down with a bit of a bump. I must have hit me chin." He continued: "I better go and make a cup of tea, I think I need one."
James made the tea and they went out of the shed premises towards the West Reading Junction goods yard. In the yard they backed onto a train of goods wagons, which had to be transported to Basingstoke goods yard.

The guard went back to the guards van, and the signal fell to give them access to the West Reading Station branch line. When they reached Southcote Junction the train was diverted onto the Basingstoke line. The engine was steaming well and James built the fire high in the firebox rear. This was his favourite method of firing and the fires glow lit up the footplate reflecting on their faces and frames. James leaned over the side of the cab and peered into the dark gloom. The fields and woods dotted along the railway embankment were obscured from the night's overcast moon. There were rain clouds scudding about the sky threatening a downpour. The train ran through Mortimer Station with John expertly driving it at a steady speed. Goods trains were restricted to a speed of about 30mph because the loose coupled wagons had no vacuum brakes. The brakes were only on the steam engine and brake van. The next station was Bramley. At Bramley there was a road crossing with a full barrier gate. The gate was open for them as they trundled through the station. As the train went past the gates the line began to rise in an adverse incline. John had to open the regulator more to combat the gradient. The big engine pulled the goods wagons with ease and they soon ran into Basingstoke goods yard. The train was uncoupled and the engine was taken into the loco depot. They then had to turn it ready for the journey back to Reading. A welcome can of tea was made in the driver's cabin.

As they sat on the footplate in the warm glow of the firebox a voice called from the ground area: "Excuse me driver. Can you give me a lift back to Reading?"
They both glanced over the side of the cab to see a young fireman standing there with the handlebars of a bicycle grasped in his hands. The voice continued: "Buggered if I want to ride back, 'cos it looks like it going to rain."
John smiled at the southern region fireman and replied: "Y-Y-Yes get up h-h-here and chuck your b-b-bike onto the tender."
The young lad climbed up into the cab and James helped pull his bicycle into the tender.

The time to leave the shed arrived and they were directed to the Basingstoke goods yard, where a train of heavily loaded coal wagons were waiting. The engine was backed onto the coal wagons, and the guard coupled them up. The guard then spoke to John saying: "You have quite a heavy load, driver. They are coal wagons for Earley Power station."
John laughed and replied: "No problem for us Great Western men," trying to impress the young Southern region fireman.

The guard ambled off into the darkness to climb into his brake van. The three enginemen waited expectantly for the red signal to turn green. The firebox glow lit up the footplate and a light rain was evident in the glow.

The Southern fireman, with a frown on his face said: "I thought it was going to rain. It's a bit of luck I can ride with you to Reading, otherwise I would have got soaked."

The goods yard signal dropped with a resounding rattle, and the red light turned green. John opened the brake ejector and wound the gear to full forward gear. The engine moved slowly forward. As they approached the line to Reading, John opened the regulator further. The coal wagons rattled noisily as their speed increased. The coal train was now picking up a rapid pace. James dropped the firebox flap and shovelled more coal into the glowing fire. He closed the flap and sat down watching the Southern fireman standing in the corner. He was intently looking out at the dark line ahead. The line dropped a significant amount as they headed towards Bramley, and James began to worry that John was forging ahead too fast for a coal train.

James was looking over the side of the cab when the distant signal for Bramley came into view. The signal was amber. This meant the signal at Bramley Station would be red. The reason for this would be that the crossing gates would be open for road traffic, but closed against them. John closed the regulator with a sharp downward movement. He then began to apply the vacuum brake, a little at a time. The wagons rattling along behind closed up buffer to buffer but failed to slow down. The train was now pushing them at a speed of at least 40mph. James wound on the tender handbrake, but he did not notice any check in the speed of the train. With a worried frown on his face John gesticulated to James to apply the tender handbrake. James grasped the brake handle and made a movement to show John he was complying, but not telling John that the brake was already wound hard to the wheels. As the train hurtled towards Bramley, completely out of control, the signal came into view.

James heaved a sigh of relief as he saw the welcome light appear green. The crossing gates were open for them and they rushed through the well-lit station platforms at an alarming speed. There was in excess of at least a thousand ton of coal wagons pushing them relentlessly toward Mortimer Station.

The young Southern fireman looked at James and whispered: "Does your driver have control of this train, mate?"

James shrugged his shoulders and whispered back: "I fucking hope so, mate!"

With both their nerves in a tizzy the two firemen watched John as he battled to retain control of the train. They were now advancing towards Southcote Junction, where the line joined the main line to London. A very busy section of rail with many fast passenger trains at all times of day and night. To their dread the distant signal for Southcote showed amber. The train was slowing gradually but not enough. The home signal for Southcote was showing red as they approached it, but they could not stop. The three of them looked up at the signal post as the engine slowly passed it.

The train came to a gratifying halt one engine and four wagon lengths past the post. John hurriedly wound the gear handle into reverse and, after lifting the regulator, he reversed the train back to the other side of the signal post.

As the engine came to a stop the Southern fireman hastily threw his bike over the side of the cab and with a cry of "Thanks for the lift," he cycled off into the darkness and safety. He must have been relieved to escape the two mad GWR men who ran coal trains so fast, like passenger trains.

John sat on his wooden seat and wrinkled his nose. "Can you smell a strange odour?" he asked James. He sniffed the air again, but James could not detect any strange smell himself. John climbed over the side of the engine, and James heard him laugh.
"Well I'm buggered. I have never seen that before," came a surprised comment. John stood beside the engine and James climbed down beside him to look at the thing amusing him. He saw the metal brake blocks on the engine were glowing red hot in the dark.
"Well I am not surprised," said James. "The brakes have been on since before Bramley."
The signal dropped and they both climbed back onto the engine. The train was taken to the Reading West Junction goods yard, where it was stood ready for a train to take it to Earley Power Station next day. After transporting the engine into Reading loco depot they left it standing in the coal stage, to be prepared for the morning. James booked off duty at 6am and as he rode home on his motorbike he thought the day had started with a hefty tumble, to end in a near disaster. He hoped that John's driving skills would improve in the near future.

IT'S A COUNTY CLASS!

The day was nice and bright with a few clouds floating about the blue sky. James mounted his BSA A7 motorbike and kicked the 500cc engine into life. The bike's twin exhausts rumbled into life and he slipped the bike into first gear. As he let out the clutch lever the bike pulled away and accelerated into a fast movement. He twisted the throttle gently as the big machine exited the Norcot council estate and surged along the Oxford Road. He relished the feel of the wind in his face as he headed towards the locomotive depot.

Today he was booked on a goods train to Swindon with Johny Eager, who was now his regular driver. After a while he pulled into Great Knollys street. Turning left he headed across the recreation ground where he shot speedily and precariously through the narrow pedestrian gate. The gap only allowed about four inches of clearance each side of the handlebars but he never considered it dangerous. After all he worked with Johny Eager!

He parked his bike and met John in the office area. The engine they had today was 6345 a Mogul type steam engine. The engine was being prepared for them and as they approached it, the driver and fireman were just completing the task. They climbed onto the footplate and the fireman spoke to James in a bold tone saying: "You got a good little engine here, mate, and I have built the fire up high in the box, should last a while."

Saying that, he climbed off the engine and headed for the drivers' cabin. His driver, who was talking to John, glanced over to James and murmured quietly: "If I were you I would push the big pricker bar through your fire because my mate, gunga bloody din has chucked in some big lumps of coal to build the fire up quick."

He winked at James and climbed off the engine to follow "gunga bloody din" to the cabin.

James made a hot can of tea and then they made their way to the Reading West Junction goods yard. The fire was burning through brightly and James ignored the driver's advice. He allowed the fire to burn through the large pieces of coal and the steam pressure built up to 200psi with no trouble. In the yard the engine was backed onto the goods wagons and the guard gave John the tally. He then retreated to the brake van. The signal to leave the yard dropped and John put the engine into full forward gear. He opened the regulator and the powerful engine hastened forward with a loud blast, promptly picking up a fast momentum. As the train moved towards the signal at Scours Lane James heaved a sigh of relief to see that the signal was green and the points set for the down relief line. He reasoned that John was moving the train too fast in a short goods spur. He thought it might be prudent to covertly apply the handbrake on the tender to slow him down in future. The journey to Swindon went without incident. They got relief in the goods yard and went into the shunters' cabin to make another can of tea. John liked his tea without sugar or milk, James considered this odd but in the future this would change.

After drinking the tea John phoned the control office to find out if they were needed to work a train back to Reading. He put the phone down and announced to James: "We h-h- have a return j-j-job, its a s-s stopping passenger train t-t-to Reading, it will be in to S-S-Swindon Station in an hour."

That settled they finished their tea, and made their way to the station. As they walked towards the station John spied a confectionery shop beside the railway embankment. He tapped James on the arm and asked: "How d-d- you fancy a n-n-nice cold ice cream?"

He then ran down the embankment and climbed over a low fence into the street. James followed him and together they finished the rest of the walk to the station slurping on ice cream cones.

On arriving at the station they made their way to number two platform. After waiting ten minutes a train appeared in the distance heading towards platform two. The engine, as it approached, shone in green livery with a polished copper top. The safety valve cover of polished brass gleamed as the train slowed to a stop.

John looked in admiration at the big engine and exclaimed: "It's a County Class!" His eyes widened with wonder.

James looked at him perplexed. "What's so special about a County Class engine?" he asked.

John replied with relish: "It's a County Class and it's got a speedometer!"

They climbed onto the spacious footplate, and James looked in admiration at the steam controls - all shiny and clean. The engine was larger than a Castle class. It also had a double blast chimney with copper tops that shone.

The fireman picked up his coat and said: "It's a great engine mate. No problems." He then climbed off the footplate and, with his driver, headed towards the station cafeteria.

James opened the firebox doors and noticed the fire was filled high in the rear of the firebox, with the coal glowing red. He raised the firebox flap and then looked over the side of the cab to watch for the guard to signal them clear to go. The guard blew his whistle and waved his green flag and climbed into his compartment.

James called to John: "Right away, mate."
John with the gear handle placed in full forward gear lifted the regulator and the engine reacted with a loud blast from the double chimney. It surged forward with a powerful movement and began to accelerate. The chimney was blasting smoke and sparks high into the air as it rushed out of the station. The train was moving at a breakneck speed as they passed the goods yards and headed towards Stratton Park Halt. John was like a child with a new toy, he was intently looking at the speedometer, unaware of the rapidly approaching stop at Stratton Park Halt. James was attending to the fire and water injectors, and as he stood up he was astonished to see the Halt flash by

He looked at his driver and shouted: "Were we not supposed to stop at that station John?"
John looked across the vibrating footplate at him and guiltily replied: "To b-b-bloody late n-n-now!" and he smiled sheepishly.
The train was now approaching Shrivenham Station. They ran into Shrivenham Station and John brought the train to a smooth halt.
As they stopped an irate guard came running along the platform towards them. With a very worried look on his face he expostulated: "What's the matter with you silly buggers? You were meant to stop at Stratton Park!"
John's face contorted in a series of grimaces as he tried to think of a sensible answer, but the guard did not wait for the answer and continued to complain. "Now I have to phone to send a taxi for the passengers at Stratton, to get them to Didcot, to catch this train there!"
He then stomped off along the platform to make the call.

John grinned at James as though he did not have a care in the world and announced: "Well we are making good time."
After the guard had made his call he signalled for them to leave. The rest of the journey was completed at a sensible speed and John remembered to halt at the arranged stations. James did not know if anybody made a complaint about the incident. John carried on as normal with no mention made of the event.

Several weeks later James and his driver John were given a simple task of relieving a goods train from Swindon and taking it to Acton goods yard. There was to be a delivery of several wagons into Drayton goods yard en route. The morning was very cold and foggy. After booking on duty at 6am they walked to the goods yard and were glad to get into the loco men's cabin for a bit of warmth. When they got into the cabin the fire in the room was not alight. James searched around the yard and found some small bits of wood to light the fire. Using a sheet of newspaper he placed the wood in the fire stove and attempted to ignite it. The wood proved to be a bit damp and James was struggling to ignite it when he spotted a bottle of what appeared to be yellow paraffin in the corner of the room. He grumbled to John: "I can't get this bloody fire lit mate. But it looks as though we are in luck, 'cos some nice person has left us a bottle of paraffin." He pointed to the bottle.

John laughed and replied: "If I were you I would take a sniff of it first to make sure its paraffin."

James picked up the bottle and unscrewed the cap. He placed it to his nose and inhaled. His face wrinkled in disgust. "Some nice person has bloody urinated in it, bit of luck I didn't chuck it on!" he said. Memories of Jack Clay came to mind; it's the rotten sort of joke he would have played.

By the time the fire was starting to burn their train arrived and they ambled over to it to relieve the crew. The engine was a 2800 class locomotive. They climbed up into the warmth of the cab, the fog was still thick and swirled about the train blocking out the view of the guard's brake van. The driver and fireman they relieved climbed on the engine and headed for the cabin, while James checked the firebox and water gauge. The fire was built high in the rear of the firebox discharging a warm glow onto the footplate. The water gauge glass was three quarters full with the steam pressure at 200psi. The coal in the tender was piled neatly and had been hosed with water to lay the dust. The footplate was comfortable and clean and James sat and admired the fireman's administrations with satisfaction. The guard they had with them was a tall chap of about 39 years of age. He looked very fit and smart in his uniform. He spoke to John saying: "Give me time to get back to the van driver 'cos you will not be able to see me in this fog."

He disappeared in the fog as he walked to the rear of the train. John waited for a while then opened the vacuum brake ejector to release the brakes. He lifted the regulator and slowly, with a gentle puff of smoke from the chimney and a hiss of steam from the piston valves, the train moved out of the yard. The journey to Slough was very slow because of the fog. John was longing to open the regulator wider to speed up the train but they rattled along at 30 miles per hour all the way to Langley Station.

At Langley the train was diverted into a goods siding to allow several passenger trains to pass them. As the line cleared the signal dropped and they pulled out of the siding and continued towards Iver Station. As the train pulled along the platform at Iver they saw the signalman leaning out of his signal box waving a red flag. John applied the brake and stopped opposite the signal box. The signalman shouted loudly to them: "YOU HAVE LEFT YOUR GUARD BEHIND AT LANGLEY!"

Confused John pushed his cap back on his head and asked: "Why, what happened to him?"

The signalman replied loudly: "HE GOT OFF TO LAY DETONATORS AT THE REAR OF YOUR TRAIN FOR PROTECTION BUT WHEN HE CAME BACK YOU HAD GONE! "HE IS RUNNING TO CATCH YOU UP, BUT YOU WILL HAVE TO CONTINUE TO WEST DRAYTON SIDINGS TO CLEAR THE LINE!"

John laughed and said to James: "Well I hope he is bloody fit 'cos it's a long run to West Drayton."

The signalman waved them on and they were diverted into the goods line to West Drayton yard. As the train ran slowly along the line John stood peering over the cab side towards a row of houses with the lights from the bedroom windows showing dimly through the fog. He mentioned to James that a very attractive young lady exhibited a dressing display in one of the bedroom windows as she clothed herself for the day.

James moved over to stand beside him not sure if it was the right thing to do but was intrigued, to say the least. As the two stood staring through the fog they became unaware of another goods train that was stationary a short distance in front of them. They suddenly realised the danger and John applied the engine's brakes but the train was not going to stop As the weight of the wagons ran into them they were pushed at a slow but steady rate towards the train's guard van. The guard must have realised they had no hope of stopping and leaped franticly out of the van. He staggered to his feet to watch helplessly as the train ran into his guard van. With an almighty loud thud his van and the whole goods train was shunted violently forwards, but came to a stop undamaged.

James was shocked by the loud collision and hoped that the engine crew on the train were not injured. After several minutes the train in front of them moved away towards Acton goods yard. When they pulled forwards into West Drayton goods yard, the shunters told them that the driver of the train was furious about the collision. He said he knew what the two idiots were doing and they should be reported. A short time after the poor knackered guard staggered into the yard to help uncouple and shunt his train into the yard. They shunted the train into the yard, and were told to take the engine to Southall loco shed. Arriving at Southall depot they drove the engine towards the coal stage area. When the engine was stopped at the coal stage area, James opened the firebox doors, and with his shovel, he lifted the heavy red hot smoke plate out. He dropped it into the coal in the tender. To his astonishment John undid his overall trousers and deliberately urinated on the red-hot metal plate. The obnoxious fumes instantly filled the air and with a laugh John climbed of the engine stuttering: "That's a p-p-parting present for S-S Southall!"

They both hurried away from the shed, which was now enveloped in the vile smell. They briskly walked to the station to catch the next train to Reading. James wondered what else was in store for his working days with John.

The day was warm with low clouds blotting out the sun, the atmosphere was humid and James did not fancy working a passenger train to Oxford. Not in this sort of weather. But this was the job allocated to John and himself today. The walk from the loco shed to Reading Station was taken at a slow amble, the excesses of the night before were telling on James. He had travelled with his drinking pal Lofty Wyatt to Twford, where they had spent the evening in the Wagon and Horses pub. The landlord was the spitting image of Alistair Sims, and he was always playing jokes on his patrons. One joke was to lower a fake spider onto the heads of any ladies sat at the bar. His wife used to play the piano and a chap used to sit next to the piano playing the drums. Lofty fancied himself as a budding Elvis Presley and after several pints of best bitter he would stand next to the piano with a microphone clasped to his mouth and try to sing. The song was *Be my teddy Bear.* Lofty used to start well and after two verses forget the words. He then used to burst out laughing and sit down embarrassed and red in the face. The night had been fun and having consumed six pints they were well and truly drunk. The trip back to Reading was in the back of a milk float, flat on their backs, thanks to a milkman friend.

So the day at work was going to be long. The walk to the station made, they waited on platform three for the Oxford train. The train was a fast passenger train to Oxford Station, where they would get relief and then work another fast passenger train to Reading. The train pulled into the station and the engine was a 4993 Dalton Hall. James loved firing the Hall class engines, they always steamed well and were comfortable to ride on. He climbed aboard the footplate and viewed the familiar surroundings. The fire was built up high to the firebox doors burning bright and hot. The steam pressure was at 220psi and the water gauge registered three quarters full. A perfect changeover he surmised. But it was too hot for comfort. The change of crew was accomplished and the signal dropped, giving them permission to continue their journey. John wound the gear handle into the full forward position and opened the regulator promptly. The train moved forward at a brisk rate with a staccato beat from the chimney.

The engine gathered speed as John adjusted the gears by winding the gear handle back. They were soon racing through Tilehurst Station with John leaning out of the cab side savouring the engine's alacrity. James fired the engine steadily and the steam pressure was easy to maintain although John was determined to go as fast as he could. With the chimney exuding a stream of smoke and steam the train ran through Didcot Station and onto the Oxford branch line. As the train passed Hinksey goods yard Oxford Station came into view. The train stopped at platform one and the relief crew climbed aboard .The train was handed over to the driver and fireman with the usual familiarities and John with James walked to the Oxford loco depot.
John looked at his watch and remarked to James: "Well mate. We have about three hours wait now. Our train to Reading is due in at 7.45pm, so shall we go to the railway social for a quiet drink?"
James agreed saying: "Yeah. Good idea, but I only want a beer shandy. I am still a bit hung over from last night."
With the time at 4pm they entered the social club and James sat in the lounge area with a shandy. Reading a book, *The Cruel Sea* by Nicholas Monsarrat, he was comfortable and at ease. John was in conversation with a couple of Oxford drivers and they decided a game of cards would pass away the time ideally.

John loved to gamble and soon money was on the table and the card game began in earnest. An hour passed and the card game was getting animated with cries of pleasure from John and groans of dismay from his opponents.
"How many times have you won, must be nearly every hand?" complained one of the Oxford drivers.
"It's 'cos I am a g-g-good p-p-pplayer," stuttered John with a grin on his face.

One of the drivers took exception to John's good mood and in an aggressive voice bleated: "I think you are cheating mate. You can't be that bloody good at cards!"
John's good mood suddenly evaporated and a scowl appeared on his face. He glared at the driver and, in a challenging tone, announced: "I will bet you a d-d-day's pay, and you c-c-can deal the c-c-cards. I don't bloody c-c-cheat!"

The Oxford driver glared at him but did not want to lose face, so he agreed to the challenge saying: "Give me the cards. Let's bloody deal them!"

The game began in a confrontational manner, both opponents grimacing with determination. Unfortunately for the Oxford driver, John won again and with a cry of victory laid the winning cards on the table. "Here you g-g-go mate f-f-full house!" He stuttered with delight.
The Oxford driver could not believe his bad luck and scrutinized the cards on the table with disappointment.
"Fuck me he's won again!" he cried in disbelief.
John held out his hand for the winning reward that the driver begrudgingly removed from his wage packet and handed to him.

The victor looked at his watch and beckoned to James asking: "Do you fancy a plate of sausage and chips mate?"
James eyes lit up with the thought of a decent meal instead of cheese and pickle sandwiches. "Thanks John. That's very nice of you, I would love a plate of chips," he smiled with pleasure, and followed his benefactor to the canteen.
The plate of sausage and chips were consumed with relish and the pair of them hastened to Oxford Station to relieve the crew of the 7.45 passenger train to Reading. The train arrived on time and James was pleased to see the engine was a Hall class again. The fireman and driver exchanged information with them and climbed off the engine to saunter off to the loco depot.

The evening light was falling and dark clouds were blotting out the little light that prevailed. James watched for the guard to give them the signal to leave. After a few minutes he waved his green flag and blew his whistle.
James called to John: "RIGHT AWAY!"
John, with his customary fast get away, pulled out of the station and the goods yard at Hinskey was soon sped by. The engine was steaming well and James only needed to fire it sparingly as they passed Appleford Station. He sat down on the hard wooden seat and surveyed the dark fields as they scooted by. The run through Didcot Station sent them onto the fast up main line towards Reading.

James stood in his corner of the footplate staring at the green signals. As they approached Cholsey Station he noticed that although all the signals were green the train was only moving at a slow pace. He peered over the dark footplate to see John seated in the wooden seat seemingly hunched over the regulator handle. He appeared motionless. James was puzzled at John's position. He looked odd. James stepped over to John and was aghast to notice he was unconscious. He reached out and grabbed John's shoulder and shook it gently enquiring with alarm: "John are you ok mate?"

There was no response and John's head slumped on his chest wobbling from side to side. James had visions of heart attack or stroke, and a feeling of panic filled his senses. "Fuck I am in trouble here!" he agonized.
With a feeling of dread, he thought how am I to drive and fire the engine? What if he is dead?

The engine was travelling along at a slow pace and James gently pushed John away from the regulator. He grasped the handle and lifted it with a jerk to gain more speed. With a jolt John's head slipped back and banged against the metal side of the cab window. His eyes opened and he enquired in a sleepy voice "Where are we?"
James heaved a sigh of relief to realise his friend and driver was still in this world and not in the next.
"Fuck! You gave me a scare John. We are at Cholsey," he scolded.
John announced with an apologetic tone in his voice: "I am alright mate. Must have dozed off. Sorry about that, I will take over now."

The journey into Reading Station went without further incidents, but James wondered how long was it that John had been asleep and it scared him.

HARRY HARBOUR AND THE 7.48 HENLEY

The winter of 1963 was a nightmare for James. Every day was a trudge to the loco depot in snow and ice. The cold artic weather did not relent and he often had to crawl under the steam engine he was preparing with a shovel loaded with burning oily waste. This was to thaw out the water feed to the injectors, which froze when the engine was parked outside the shed.

One morning he was rostered to work on the 7.48am Henley with driver Harry Harbour. He arrived to work early, as was his normal practice when having to prepare an engine. He arrived in the dark winter morning with snow and icy winds making him shudder. The engine allocated to them today was 7032 Denbigh Castle. James looked at the big engine and admired the shining green bodywork. The copper top band around the chimney shone in the light of the shed's dull illumination, as did the bright yellow burnished safety valve cover.

He began to prepare the engine with alacrity in an attempt to keep warm. By the time Harry arrived he had nearly finished the preparation and was cleaning the footplate area. Harry climbed onto the engine and greeted him with a curt good morning and went off to collect his oil. James cleaned the footplate. He polished the faceplate of all coal dust and had it looking clean and comfortable when Harry returned to begin his oiling routine.
Harry looked at James and asked in a concerned tone: "Has my fireman arrived yet?"
James replied in a surprised response: "I am your fireman for today Harry."
Harry stared at the young looking fireman and, in a more concerned tone, inquired: "Have you done this job before then?"
James grinned at Harry's nervous question and replied with: "No mate. It's all new to me."
He watched Harry's face become crestfallen as he lied to him. James had worked the 7.48 Henley train several times. He knew it was an important train for the Reading men as a lot of people who worked in Paddington and the London area used it. Harry muttered to him: "Well make sure you have a good fire in the firebox 'cos this job is important."

With the dark cold morning enveloping them they made their way to the exit signal at the Reading Station end of the shed. The signal dropped and the big Denbigh Castle 7032, with a full haycock fire, glided through Reading Station on its way to Henley.

James, who was aware of Harry's concern, continued to fire the engine as they approached Twyford Station. The bright glow illuminated the footplate and added a warmth to its occupants but it also caused the steam pressure to rise above what was required. Trying to keep it below 225psi was becoming a problem, and the safety valve was showing a feather of steam as they ran tender first into Henley. James closed the ash pan dampers while they steam heated the train. This kept the steam pressure down. The train was backed into the station at the required time and James opened the dampers and added more coal into the firebox. Harry was still nervously watching his fireman and his fireman was nervously watching his steam pressure. It was rising to 225psi - the safety valve optimum. James opened the water injector and fed water into the boiler. This lowered the pressure but also overfilled the boiler. He knew that if the boiler was overfilled the water would carry over with the steam and into the cylinders. This created a hydraulic effect of water being ejected out of the chimney. Not good practice.

The guard eventually gave them the green flag and Harry lifted the regulator. The big green Castle class engine pulled out of the station with a series of muffled blasts from the chimney. James winced as he realised the water level in the boiler was too high. But Harry was insisting he kept the fire high so he shovelled a few more lumps of coal into the back end of the firebox. The run to Shiplake was speedily accomplished with the anxious fireman sitting watching the water gauge and steam pressure. The safety valve hissed gently but did not lift completely. As they pulled out of the station the engine responded with a sharp number of blasts from the chimney. James sighed with relief as he realised the water level in the boiler was now at its correct working level. Running into Wargrave Station Harry brought the train to a professional slow halt and the steam pressure was just below the 225psi mark. James opened the water injector and fed more water into the boiler. The steam pressure dropped to 220psi with James now satisfied that the engine was operating perfectly. As they ran into Twyford Station the steam pressure was 220psi and the water gauge showed three quarters full. James thought he now had it under control and Harry seemed more relaxed.

The big engine pulled out of Twyford Station with an encouraging series of blasts of coal smoke and steam. The hydraulic effect had diminished since leaving Henley and the train gathered speed competently. The run from Twyford was quite long and James added more coal into the firebox to keep Harry satisfied. He was still muttering something about keeping a good fire in the box. The steam pressure was remaining at 220psi. But when Harry closed the regulator to slow down for Maidenhead Station the steam pressure suddenly escalated sharply. As the train ran into the station the safety valve lifted with a roar of steam and water.

Because the boiler was overfull the safety valve ejected water as well as steam. The passengers on the platform were subjected to a shower of chalky coloured water as the train ran into the station. James looked at their smart dark rain macs and overcoats and hoped the chalky water would not bring forth any complaints. He hoped Harry would stop complaining and worrying as the engine was steaming superbly and they were keeping time easily. As the train stood in the station the safety valve still hissed and spluttered with a noise that the passengers could hear and wonder about. When they got the right away from the guard Harry lifted the regulator and as the engine pulled away from the station the safety valve closed. The big Castle class engine picked up speed effortlessly and they passed Taplow and Burham at great rapidity. The big wheels of the engine were soon thundering through Slough Station, and as Langley Station came into view James leaned over the side of the cab and thought of the day they left the guard behind. He chuckled at the reminder of the poor guard running to catch them up. Then the row of houses appeared as they hurtled towards West Drayton. This was where John had run into the rear of the stationary goods train. The speed they were now traveling at made the footplate vibrate. But as the train ran through Southall Station the ride was perfect compared to the horrendous ride they had on the engine with the flat wheel.

The rest of the run into Paddington went without a worry and they ran into the platform on time, with the fire low enough to keep the safety valve closed. Harry did not complain the rest of the day and ceased worrying. The silly old sod.

63 WINTER SNOW.

James pulled the bedcovers back over his head and revelled in the warmth of the bed. He knew that outside of the frost covered windows lay a scene of frozen hostility. The snow had started to fall on Boxing Day night - 26th December 1962. It was now Monday 31st of December and still the snow was still falling. He now had a young wife and two young children to support, so the thought of remaining in the comfort of this warm room was a forgotten dream. He was due in work at 7am to work an empty coal train to Swindon. The light outside the window was dark but the snow added light reflections from the streetlights.

He climbed out of the warm bed and pulled the curtains to view the clean white snow piling up in the roadway. He groaned with dismay at the thought of having to prepare a steam locomotive in these harsh conditions. He turned on the radio to hear the rock n roll sound of Elvis Presley singing *Return to Sender*, if only he could do that with the bloody snow. He hurriedly got dressed and added a thick woollen sweater under his overalls. That, he thought, would be sufficient to keep out the chill wind that was creating snowdrifts along the railway embankments.

With the rest of the house in silent darkness, and with his great coat pulled on over his jacket he opened the front door. He stepped out into the cold morning air looking like a padded dummy. The walk to the locomotive shed did not take long as he was now living in Greyfriars Road opposite Reading Station. As he trudged past the Reading West signal box he left footprints in the pristine snow that covered the boardwalk. When he reached the loco depot he booked on duty, and after collecting two lamps from the lamp house made his way to a 2800 locomotive parked at the rear of the shed. The engine was stationed on number nine pit and had a fine layer of snow covering it. James climbed onto the snow-covered footplate, cursing the lack of cover on these engines. He hoped that there may be a tarpaulin in the toolbox but when he opened the snow-covered lid he was disappointed to find it empty. Probably emptied by another fireman seeking extra cover and warmth. He scrambled up on the front of the engine to inspect the smoke box. He was careful to avoid the slippery frozen metal surface, as his studded army boots were lethal in this weather. Satisfied all was well he closed the smoke box door and swept the snow from the front of the engine. Quite a futile attempt he reckoned as it was very soon replaced, as the wind blew more flurries of snow into his face. He quickly returned to the cab and its limited comfort.

Johny Eager climbed onto the footplate covered in flakes of snow and greeted him with a grin saying: "Lovely bit of weather mate. Very fresh morning eh?" James smiled and commented: "You look like the snow fairy John."
John, with his normal good humour not disturbed by the weather conditions, continued to oil the engine's frozen rods and links. James lifted the long metal pricker bar from the tender and spread the burning coal over the firebox. The coal ignited and soon he had a decent hot blaze raising the steam pressure in the boiler. He continued to shovel more coal into the blaze until it was high in the rear of the box, radiating extra warmth into the cab. He then trimmed the tender coal pile, breaking the large lumps of coal into fist-size manageable lumps. When he completed the trimming he hosed the footplate clean and then made his way to the driver's cabin to make a welcome cup of hot tea.

Sitting in the warmth of the cab they drank the hot tea with relish, the warm nectar very much appreciated. James groped in his lunch bag to withdraw a small bottle of whiskey. He furtively poured a small amount into his cup and said to John: "Would you care for an extra warming liquid John?"
He waved the small bottle of whiskey towards John. The driver's eyes lit up and he replied: "I would love a drop of your liquid. How could I refuse?" He held out his cup for James to drop the golden warm liquid into. James could feel the warmth of the tea coursing through his insides being greatly accepted. Anything to keep out the numbing cold he thought.

With both driver and fireman now fortified against the chill air they made their way to the exit signal at the east end of the shed. The signalman dropped the signal and they reversed through Reading Station to back onto a train of empty coal wagons. These were in the yard by Reading gas works. The guard standing forlornly in the cold snow coupled them to the wagons and beat a hasty retreat to his warm brake van.

They sat and waited for the signal that would give them access to the main line through Reading Station. The signal dropped and John lifted the regulator. The big 2800 engine, giving a series of loud blasts of smoke and steam, pulled the frozen wagons briskly up the line to Reading Station. As they went through the station they were directed onto the down relief line and were soon trundling through a frozen Tilehurst Station. The snow continued to fall with a harsh north wind battering the engine and empty coal wagons.

Passenger trains were hurtling past them with snow piled on the carriage roofs. One passenger train was white with frost and snow. The windows were obscured with layers of white frost, with icicles hanging from the sides, making the train look a ghostly spectacle. Obviously the heating from the engine must have failed, creating gross discomfort to the poor passengers, thought James.

The artic wind was blowing into the side of the cab now, carrying with it flurries of snow. James reached for his great coat that was hanging on the side of the cab. He pulled it on to help reduce the numbing wind. But he now found it difficult to bend his body to facilitate the firing of the engine. He removed the coat again and shovelled more coal into the firebox. He looked at John sitting with only his small jacket on, seemingly oblivious to the artic conditions. The train was now moving at a hurried pace as they neared Didcot Station. James stealthily wound on the tender handbrake hoping John would not notice. It had become a habit since the West Drayton episode. He did not want to repeat that in a hurry.

John was still lifting the regulator as the train ran through the station, muttering to himself: "This engine's bloody sluggish today mate!" But James did not release the handbrake, as he knew they would be directed into the goods line a little further on.

The landscape and embankments were piled high with snow and ice as they neared Steventon goods loop. The signal for the goods loop dropped and John, still grumbling about its sluggish response, braked the train to a slow pace as it traversed the points into the line. They slowly ran up to the exit signal and came to a stop. The biting chill wind blew snow across the fields piling it up high in the loop line. James sneakily opened his small whiskey bottle and took a swig. The whiskey was not a taste he enjoyed but the heated feeling as it slipped into his chilled frame was bliss. He offered John a sip, which he thankfully consumed as the artic wind was piling more snow into the tender and cab. They sat with the firebox flap lowered to gain some heat from the fire. The sound of loud voices cut through the silence of the loop.

Looking over the side of the cab James spotted a party of six grey figures plodding through the snow at the side of the wagons. They drew level with the engine and a person looked up at him and proclaimed in a hoarse voice: "We have come to dig you out mate. The points are buried and frozen, it may take a while!"

The six burly figures carrying big snow shovels walked to the front of the engine and began to laboriously dig at the snow mound. John glanced over the cab side and in a stuttering voice said: "I d-d-don't envy those ch-ch-chaps. Are you g-g-going to help them?"

James grinned at the silly remark and responded with a laugh: "Like hell I am. It's not in my contract!" He leaned nearer the firebox opening. The sound of the arduous shovelling came to a halt and the signal dropped to allow them access to the main line. James closed the firebox flap as John lifted the regulator, and with the engine wheels slipping slightly they pulled the frozen wagons free from the loop line. James leaned over the side of the cab and waved a thank you to the grey figures. They leaned on their shovels and waved back to him, probably glad to see him go.

The train gained speed with John opening the regulator wider to attempt to gain even more speed. James had released the handbrake but John did not seem to notice how the sluggishness had stopped. The white covered fields and hedges sped by as the train rattled along towards Challow. The snow was still falling and the embankments were piling even higher with the snow clinging to them. They passed Uffington with the white horse on the hill obliterated from view as the snow buried its white form. They ran into Shrivenham with the signals at green and were shortly running into the Swindon goods yard. As the train came to a halt James headed to the shunters' cabin to brew a can of hot tea. The snow was getting deeper as it intermittently came down hard. The whole area was white and clean with the snow cover. He clambered back onto the footplate and they both drank the hot tea secretly laced with the remaining whiskey. Their relief crew ambled across to them several minutes later. The two frozen bodies swiftly headed to the shunters' cabin to sample its warm interior and. report to the control staff.

The control asked them if they would take a goods train on to Banbury. The train would be arriving about haft an hour later in the Swindon up goods loop. James was not anxious to go to Banbury, knowing the line had a lot of bad inclines, and memories of the Basingstoke fiasco still filled his mind. John was enthusiastic about the chance to make a few hours overtime but James reluctantly disagreed. John realised that due to the bad winter conditions the run to Banbury would take a long time. He phoned the control room and asked if there were any goods trains going to Reading. The reply was no, so they made their way to the station to catch the next passenger train going to Reading Station The need to ride in a warm carriage was paramount in James' mind. He did not realise that the freezing artic conditions would last for another two months. There were a lot of cold trips to experience later.

The winter of 1963 continued with snow and ice for three months. It started snowing on the 26th of December and continued until March. The cold harsh conditions were not horrendous but a bloody nuisance, thought James. He now had a wife and two children and as the weather got warmer in March he fell ill with influenza. Now when someone gets a cold virus they bleat that they have the flu. No they do not have the flu. The flu is a debilitating illness that knocks you bandy. It lays you out flat with awful aches, chills and sweats. James suddenly felt ill on a Saturday evening and took to his bed where he stayed incumbent for six days. He could not eat anything without being nauseous. He could not drink anything but Lucozade. He lay in his bed as weak as a kitten. After a week of misery and pain he returned to work. He went to the pay office and enquired if he would receive sick pay. The answer was an emphatic "no". When he asked why, the answer was that he did not have enough years of service to comply. He was absolutely astounded by British Rail's sickness policy. In the eight years he had worked for the company he had never gone sick. Now when he needed sick pay it was refused. To say he was fuming with indignation was mild. He was furious and resentful to be treated this way, and the writing was on the wall for him to give notice of employment. He carried on working for British Rail until the August, but with a heavy heart. He now lacked any enthusiasm for the work or the engines. The pay for a 44-hour week was £13 but Gillettes were offering £18 for a 60 hour week. So James joined the staff of Gillettes in the Basingstoke Road. To his surprise he met the guard who got left behind at Langley, working in the Needles department. He probably lost interest in British rail also.

RIPLEY ROAD READING 1950 ERA

READING LOCO SHED 1950s

ALFIE BOTTIN ON THE COAL STAGE 1956

4950 PATSHULL HALL ON THE COAL STAGE 1950s ERA

6120 ON THE TURNTABLE 1950s ERA

LOFTY BILL WYATT ON HUTTON HALL 1956

BOOKING ON DUTY AT READING LOCO SHED 1950s ERA

BILL [chinky] GOODAL ON THE FOOTPLATE

HALL CLASS LOCO AT OXFORD LOCO SHED COAL STAGE AREA

READING LOCO SHED 1950s

BULLDOG LOCO 1940s AT READING

READING LOCO SHED DRIVERS AND FIREMEN 1948 JOE LEE 4TH FROM RIGHT BACK ROW

CASTLE CLASS LOCO BEING PREPARED FOR SERVICE AT READING LOCO SHED 1960s ERA

DRIVER JOE LEE

READING LOCO DEPOT 1958

GOODS TRAIN WITH A 2800 LOCO ENTERING READING STATION

PIC OF READING SHED DEVOIN OF LOCOMOTVES 1964

PIC COLEY BRANCH TRAIN HEADING TOWARDS READING WEST JUNCTION YARD

JAMES AND JOHNY EAGERS ON GLADIATOR IN READING STATION 1961

JAMES READY FOR THE FRAY 1956

READING LOCO SHED 1950s ERA

GEORGE GOODAL AND HIS BROTHER BOTH LOCOMOTIVE FIREMEN AT READING 1956

FAST PASSENGER TRAIN LEAVING READING STATION HEADING WEST

READING LOCO SHED 1950s

ENTRANCE TO READING LOCO SHED FROM GT KNOLLYS STREET

READING LOCO SHED WEST SIDE

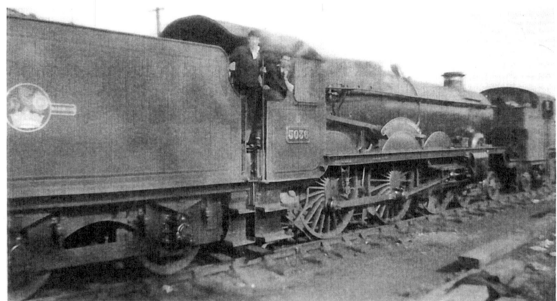

BILL (LOFTY) WYATT ON 5036 LYONSHALL CASTLE AT READING LOCO 1955